Philosophical Inquiries

PHILOSOPHICAL INQUIRIES

An Introduction to Problems of Philosophy

Nicholas Rescher

UNIVERSITY OF PITTSBURGH PRESS

Published by the University of Pittsburgh Press, Pittsburgh, Pa., 15260
Copyright © 2010, University of Pittsburgh Press
All rights reserved
Manufactured in the United States of America
Printed on acid-free paper
10 9 8 7 6 5 4 3 2 1

Library of Congress Cataloging-in-Publication Data

Rescher, Nicholas.
    Philosophical inquiries : an introduction to problems of philosophy / Nicholas
Rescher.
        p. cm.
    Includes bibliographical references (p.   ) and index.
    ISBN 978-0-8229-6075-1 (pbk. : alk. paper)
 1.   Philosophy—Introductions.   I. Title.
    BD21.R47 2010
    100—dc22   2010002372

For John Leslie

CONTENTS

Preface ix

1. The Task of Philosophy   1
2. Knowledge and Scepticism   20
3. Limits of Science   36
4. Realism/Idealism   51
5. Intelligent Design   61
6. Fallacies Regarding Free Will   74
7. Mind and Matter   89
8. Pragmatism and Practical Rationality   98
9. The Demands of Morality   110
10. By Whose Standards?   132
11. Pluralism and Concretization Quandaries   146
12. The Power of Ideals   158
13. Science and Religion   170
14. On the Improvability of the World   189
15. Why Philosophy?   201

Notes   207

Index of Names   217

PREFACE

Before getting down to the book's proper work, a brief preliminary word about the nature of the enterprise is in order. This book is compiled in the spirit of Bertrand Russell's *Problems of Philosophy* and A. J. Ayer's *Central Questions in Philosophy* as an attempt by a senior philosopher to give a sort of cook's tour conspectus of major philosophical issues. It is not a students' introduction to philosophy, nor does it seek to provide a comprehensive survey of the field—no single volume could hope to do this, let alone such a brief one. Rather, the object is to give an instructive panorama of one philosopher's views on some of the major issues of the field. And so, it is hoped, that the book succeeds in presenting a series of readily comprehensive studies of significant philosophical issues that manage to convey some of one particular philosopher's ideas on key issues in an informative and accessible way.

I am very grateful to Estelle Burris for her ever-competent assistance in preparing this material for the press.

Philosophical Inquiries

1

The Task of Philosophy

The Nature of Philosophy as a Cognitive Enterprise

Philosophy may well be something of an acquired taste. For philosophers not only raise questions and propose answers, but they try to glimpse behind the curtain of such issues. They want to question the questions themselves and ask why they are important. And they are not just satisfied to have an answer but want to know just what it is that makes an answer correct and appropriate.

Philosophy is identified as one particular human enterprise among others by its characterizing mission of providing satisfactory answers to the "big questions" that we have regarding the world's scheme of things and our place within it. Often as not, those big questions in philosophy are *explanatory* questions, questions whose answers "explain the facts," thereby enabling us to understand why things are as they indeed are. The history of philosophy is an ongoing intellectual struggle to develop ideas that render comprehensible the seemingly endless diversity and complexity that surrounds us on all sides. The instruments of philosophizing are the ideational resources of concepts and theories, and philosophy deploys them in a quest for understanding, in the endeavor to create an edifice of thought able to provide us with an intellectual home that affords a habitable shelter in a complicated and challenging world. As a venture in providing rationally cogent answers to our questions about large-scale issues regarding belief, evaluation, and action, philosophy is a sector of the cognitive enterprise at large. And subsidiarily—since a rational creature acts on the basis of its beliefs—philosophy also has a bearing on action so as to implement the idea of *philou phliu blou kubernetes*—the motto of the American Phi Beta Kappa Society, which has it that philosophy is a guide to life.

Philosophy has no distinctive information sources of its own. It has its own *problems*, but the *substantive raw materials* by whose means it develops answers must ultimately come from elsewhere. It thus has no distinctive subject matter to separate it from other branches of inquiry and furnishes no novel facts but only offers insights into relationships. For *everything* is relevant to its concerns, its tasks being to provide a sort of *expositio mundi*, a traveler's guidebook to reality at large. The mission of philosophy is to ask, and to answer in a rational and disciplined way, all those great questions about life in this world that people wonder about in their reflective moments.

In the first book of the *Metaphysics*, Aristotle tells us that "it is through wonder that men now begin and originally began to philosophize, wondering in the first place at obvious perplexities, and then by gradual progression raising question about the greater matters too, for example, about the origin of the universe."[1] And this characterization of the field is right on target. Philosophy strives after that systematic integration of knowledge that the sciences initially promised but have never managed to deliver because of their increasing division of labor and never-ending pursuit of specialized detail. For what philosophy endeavors (or *should* endeavor) to do is to look at the sum total of what we know and tell us what it means for us—where the moral lies ("die Moral von der Geschicht"). Dealing with being and value in general—with possibility, actuality, and worth—the concerns of philosophy are universal and all-embracing. And not only is philosophy too inclusive and all encompassing to have a restricted range of concern, but it also does not have any altogether distinctive method. Its procedures of inquiry and reasoning are too varied and diversified, making use in this endeavor of whatever useful means come to hand for exclusivity—it takes what it needs from whatever source it can. What characterizes philosophy is thus neither a special subject matter nor a special methodology but rather—to reemphasize—its defining mission is that of coordinating the otherwise available information in the light of big questions regarding man, the world, and his place within its scheme of things. Philosophy deals largely with *how* and *whether* and *why* questions: how the world's arranged, how it stand in relation to us, whether things are as they seem, and why things should be as they are (for example, why it is that we should do "the ethically right" things). Ever since Socrates pestered his fellow Athenians with puzzling issues about "obvious" facts regarding truth and justice, philosophers have probed for the reason why behind the reason why.

Philosophy's question-oriented concerns address three sorts of issues in particular:

- *informative* (determining what is the case)
- *practical* (how to do things: how to achieve our aims)
- *evaluative/directive* (what to aim at)

It is the "big issues" in these three cases with which philosophy concerns itself. And it must be systematic because it must—for reasons we shall soon examine more closely—deal with the vast image of issues in an integrated, consistent, and coherent way. Philosophy is quintessentially the work of reason. The aim of the enterprise is to provide rational coherence to our thoughts and rational direction to our actions.

After all, it is clearly not just answers that we want, but answers whose tenability can plausibly be established—rationally defensible and well-substantiated answers. And in particular, this requires that we transact our question-resolving business in a way that is harmonious with and does not damage our prephilosophical connections in matters of everyday life and scientific inquiry. Philosophy's mandate is to answer questions in a manner that achieves overall rational coherence so that the answers we give to some of our questions square with those that we give to others.

Philosophy is matter of rational inquiry, a cognitive enterprise, a venture in question-resolution subject to the usual standards of rationality. In doing philosophy we are committed by the very nature of the project at hand to maintaining a commitment to the usual ground rules of cognitive and practical rationality.[2]

To be sure, we are sometimes said to be living in a post-philosophical age—an era when the practice of philosophy is no longer viable. But this is absurd. Nowadays more than ever we both desire and require the guidance of rigorous thinking about the nature of the world and our place within it. And the provision of such an intellectual orientation is philosophy's defining mission. The fact is that the impetus to philosophy lies in our very nature as rational inquirers: as beings who have questions, demand answers, and want these answers to be cogent ones. Cognitive problems arise when matters fail to meet our expectations, and the expectation of rational order is the most fundamental of them all. The fact is simply that we *must* philosophize; it is a situational imperative for a rational creature.

The Need for Philosophy: Humans as *Homo quaerens*

At the basis of the cognitive enterprise lies the fact of human curiosity rooted in the need-to-know of a weak and vulnerable creature emplaced in a difficult and often hostile environment in which it must make its evolutionary way by its wits. For we must act—our very survival depends upon it—and a rational animal must align its actions with its beliefs. We have a very real and material stake in securing viable answers to our questions as to how things stand in the world we live in.

The discomfort of unknowing is a natural human sentiment. To be ignorant of what goes on about one is unpleasant to the individual and dangerous to the species from an evolutionary point of view. As William James wisely observed:

> The utility of this emotional affect of expectation is perfectly obvious; "natural selection," in fact, was bound to bring it about sooner or later. It is of the utmost practical importance to an animal that he should have prevision of the qualities of the objects that surround him.[3]

There is good reason why we humans pursue knowledge—it is our evolutionary destiny. Humans have evolved within nature to fill the ecological niche of an intelligent being. We are neither numerous and prolific (like the ant and the termite), nor tough and aggressive (like the shark). Weak and vulnerable creatures, we are constrained to make our evolutionary way in the world by the use of brainpower. It is by knowledge and not by hard shells or sharp claws or keen teeth that we have carved out our niche in evolution's scheme of things. The demand for understanding, for a cognitive accommodation to one's environment, for "knowing one's way about," is one of the most fundamental requirements of the human condition. Our questions form a big part of our life's agenda, providing the impetus that gives rise to our knowledge—or putative knowledge—of the world. Our species is *Homo quaerens*. We have questions and want (nay, *need*) answers.

In situations of cognitive frustration and bafflement we cannot function effectively as the sort of creature nature has compelled us to become. Confusion and ignorance—even in such "remote" and "abstruse" matters as those with which philosophy deals—yield psychic dismay and discomfort. The old saying is perfectly true: philosophy bakes no bread. But it is also no less true that man does not live by bread alone. The physical side of our nature that impels us to eat, drink, and be merry is just one of its sides. *Homo sapiens* require nourishment for the mind as urgently as nourishment for the body. We seek knowledge not only because we wish, but because we must. For us humans, the need for information, for knowledge to nourish the mind, is every bit as critical as the need for food to nourish the body. Cognitive vacuity or dissonance is as distressing to us as hunger or pain. We want and need our cognitive commitments to comprise an intelligible story, to give a comprehensive and coherent account of things. Bafflement and ignorance—to give suspensions of judgment the somewhat harsher name they deserve—exact a substantial price from us. The quest for cognitive orientation in a difficult world represents a deeply practical requisite for us. The basic demand for information and understanding presses in upon us, and we must do (and are pragmatically justified in doing) what is needed for its satisfaction. For us, cognition is the most practical of matters. Knowledge itself fulfills an acute practical need. And this is where philosophy comes in, in its attempt to grapple with our basic cognitive concerns.

Philosophy seeks to bring rational order, system, and intelligibility to the confusing diversity of our cognitive affairs. It strives for orderly arrangements in the cognitive sphere that will enable us to find our way about in the world in an effective and satisfying way. Philosophy is indeed a venture in theorizing, but one whose rationale is eminently practical. A rational animal that has to make its evolutionary way in the world by its wits has a deep-rooted need for speculative reason.

But why pursue rationalizing philosophy at all—why accept this enterprise as an arena of appropriate human endeavor? The answer is that it is an integral and indispensable component of the larger project of rational inquiry regarding issues important to us humans. This, to be sure, simply pushes the question back: why pursue reasoned inquiry? And this question splits into two components.

The first component is: Why pursue *inquiry?* Why insist on knowing about things and understanding them? The answer is twofold. On the one hand, knowledge is its own reward. And on the other hand, knowledge is the indispensable instrument for the more efficient and effective realization of other goals. We accordingly engage in philosophical inquiry because we must; because those great intellectual issues of man and his place in the world's scheme, of the true and the beautiful and the good, of right and wrong, freedom and necessity, causality and determinism, and so on, matter greatly to us—to all of us some of the time and to some of us all of the time. We philosophize because it is important to us to have answers to our questions. After all, a philosophical work is neither a work of fiction nor a work of history. Its mission is not so much to enlighten or to inform as to persuade: to convince people of the appropriateness of a certain solution to a certain problem. What is at issue is, at bottom, an exercise in question resolution—in problem solving. Its roots are in human curiosity—in the "facts of life," that we have questions and may need to obtain cognitively satisfying answers to them.

The second component of our question is: why *reasoned* inquiry? The answer is that we are *Homo sapiens*, a *rational* animal. We do not want just answers, but answers that can satisfy the demands of our intelligence—answers that we can in good conscience regard as appropriate, as tenable, and defensible. We are not content with information about which answers people would like to have (psychologism), nor with information about what sort of answers are available (possibility mongering). What we want is cogent guidance regarding which answers to *adopt*—which contentions are correct or, at any rate, plausible. And reason affords our prime standard in this regard.

Philosophy, then, is an inquiry that seeks to resolve problems arising from the incoherence of the matter of our extraphilosophical commitments. And to abandon philosophy is to rest content with incoherence. One can, of course, cease to do philosophy (and this is what sceptics of all persuasions have always wanted). But if one is going to philosophize at all, one has no alternative but to proceed by means of arguments and inferences, the traditional vehicles of human rationality.

Yet, why pursue such a venture in the face of the all too evident possibility of error? Why run such cognitive risks? For it is only too clear that there *are* risks here. In philosophizing, there is a gap between the individual indications at our disposal and the answers to our questions that we decide to accept. (As there also is in science—but in philosophy the gap is far wider because the questions are of a different scale.) Because of this, the positions we take have to be held tentatively, subject to expectation of an almost certain need for amendment, qualification, improvement, and modification. Philosophizing in the classical manner—exploiting the available indications of experience to answer those big questions on the agenda of traditional philosophy—is predicated on the use of reason to do the best we can to align our cognitive commitments with the substance of our experience. In this sense, philosophizing involves an act of faith: when we draw on our experience to answer our questions we have to proceed in the tentative hope that the best we can do is good enough, at any rate, for our immediate purposes.

The question of intellectual seriousness is pivotal here. Do we care? Do we *really want* answers to our questions? And are we sufficiently committed to this goal to be willing to take risks for the sake of its achievement—risks of potential error, of certain disagreement, and of possible philistine incomprehension? For these risks are un-avoidable—an ineliminable part of the philosophical venture. If we lose the sense of legitimacy and become too fainthearted to run such risks, we must pay the price of abandoning the inquiry.

This of course can be done. But to abandon the quest for answers in a *reasoned* way is impossible. For in the final analysis there is no alternative to philosophizing as long as we remain in the province of reason. We adopt some controversial position or other, no matter which way we turn— no matter how elaborately we try to avoid philo-sophical controversy—it will come back to haunt us. The salient point was already well put by Aristotle: "[Even if we join those who believe that philosophizing is not possible] in this case too we are obliged to inquire how it is possible for there to be no Philosophy; and then, in inquiring, we philosophize, for rational inquiry is the essence of Phi-losophy."[4] To those who are prepared simply to abandon philosophy, to withdraw from the whole project of trying to make sense of things, we can have nothing to say. (How can one reason with those who deny the point and propriety of reasoning?) But with those who *argue* for its abandonment we can do something—once we have enrolled them in the community as fellow theorists with a position of their own. F. H. Bradley hit the nail on the head: "The man who is ready to prove that metaphysical knowledge is impossible . . . is a brother metaphysician with a rival theory of first principles."[5] One can aban-don philosophy, but one cannot *advocate* its abandonment through rational argumentation without philosophizing.

The question, "should we philosophize?" accordingly receives a straightforward answer: the impetus to philosophize lies in our very nature as rational inquirers. We must philosophize; it is a situational imperative for a rational creature such as ourselves.

Rationality is the Instrument of Philosophy

The ancients saw man as "the rational animal," set apart from other creatures by capacities for speech and deliberation. Under the prec-edent of Greek philosophy, Western thinkers have generally deemed the use of thought for the guidance of our proceedings to be at once the glory and the duty of *Homo sapiens*.

Rationality consists in the intelligent pursuit of appropriate ends. It calls for the appropriate use of reason to resolve choices in the best possible way. To behave rationally is to make use of one's intelligence to figure out the best thing to do in the circumstances. It is a matter of the recognizably effective pursuit of appropriately appreciated benefits. Rationality thus has a crucially economic dimension, seeing that the impetus to economize is an inherent part of intelligent comportment. Rationality is a matter of deliberately doing the best one can with the means at one's disposal—of striving for the best results that one can expect to achieve within the range of one's resources—specifically including one's intellectual resources. Optimization in what one thinks, does, and values is the crux of rationality. Costs and benefits are the pivotal factors. Be it in matters of belief, action, or evaluation, rationality demands a deliberate endeavor to optimize benefits relative to the expenditure of available resources. Reason requires the cultivation of intelligently adopted objectives in intelligent ways.

Rationality is not an inevitable feature of conscious organic life. Here on earth, at least, it is our specifically human instrumentality, a matter of our particular evolutionary heritage. Rational intelligence—the use of our brains to guide action by figuring out what is the apparent best—is the survival instrument of our species, in much the same way that other creatures have managed to ensure their survival by being prolific, or tough, or well sheltered. It is a means to adaptive efficiency, enabling us—sometimes at least—to adjust our environment to our needs and wants rather than conversely.

The maintenance of rational coherence and consistency is a key task of philosophy. But is such consistency itself not simply a mere ornament, a dispensable luxury, the hobgoblin of little minds? Rousseau wrote to one of his correspondents that he did not wish to be shackled by narrow-minded consistency—he proposed to write whatever seemed sensible at the time. In a writer of belles lettres, this sort of flexibility may seem refreshingly open-minded. But such an approach is not available to a philosopher. Philosophy in its very nature is a venture of systematization and rationalization—of rendering matters intelligible and accessible to rational thought. Its concern is for the rational order and systemic coherence of our commitments. The commitment to rational coherence is a part of what makes philosophy the enterprise it is.

But why not embrace contradiction in a spirit of openness rather than flee from it?[6] The answer is that rejecting inconsistencies is the only road to comprehension and understanding. To the extent that we do not resolve an issue in one definite way to the exclusion of others, we do not resolve it at all. Only a coherent, alternative-excluding resolution is a resolution at all. Moreover, intelligence has for us, an evolutionary dimension, and only a consistent and coherent mode of action can provide for evolutionary efficacy.

The presence of an inconsistency in framing an answer to a question is self-destructive. To respond "yes *and* no" is in effect to offer no response at all; answers that do not *exclude* manage to achieve no useful *inclusions* either. Only where some possibilities are denied is anything asserted: "All determination is negation" (*omnis affirmatio est negatio*). A logically inconsistent theory of something is thereby self-defeating—not just because it affirms an impossibility but because it provides no information on the matter at issue. An inconsistent "position" is no position at all. Keeping on good terms with *all* the possibilities requires that we embrace none. But the point of having a position at all is to have some answer to some question or other. If we fail to resolve the problem in favor of one possibility or another, we do not have an answer. To whatever extent we fail to resolve the issue in favor of one alternative or another, we also fail to arrive at some answer to the question. Ubiquitous yea-saying is socially accommodating but informatively unhelpful. (Compare Aristotle's defense of the law of noncontradiction in Book Gamma of the *Metaphysics*.) As long as and to the extent that inconsistencies remain, our goal of securing information or achieving understanding is defeated.

To be sure, while we ever strive to *improve* our knowledge, we never manage to *perfect* it. The stage for our present deliberations is itself set by a trio of individually plausible but collectively incompatible theses represented by the inconsistent triad:

1. Reality is knowable. (Thought can adequately characterize reality—not fully, to be sure, but at any rate in essentials.)

2. Our knowledge of reality is consistent; it constitutes a logically "coherent whole." Rational inquiry can in principle depict reality adequately in a coherent system of true propositions.

3. Experience shows that our ventures at devising knowledge of reality eventually run into inconsistency as we work out their ramifications and implications more fully.

Such an aporetic cluster of inconsistent plausibilities comes to be resolved by abandoning one of the theses involved.

Now denial of thesis 3 is not a promising option here since, to all appearances, this simply represents a "fact of life" regarding the situation in philosophy. Rejecting 2 also has its problems. Perhaps it is conceivable (just barely) that reality will, whenever offered a choice of alternatives, decide to have it both ways and accept inconsistency—a prospect envisaged by thinkers from the days of Nicholas of Cusa to contemporary neo-Hegelians. This is a theory that we might, in the end, feel compelled to adopt. But clearly only as a last resort, "at the end of the day"—and thus effectively never. In philosophy, we want to make sense of things. A theory that says they just cannot be made sense of coherently and consistently may well have various merits, but it is nevertheless decisively flawed. Its defect is not just a lack of rationality but a lack of utility as well. For such a theory simply aborts the aim of the cognitive enterprise—it impedes any prospect of gathering information.

And so, denying thesis 1 affords the most readily available option. We must concede that philosophical thought can at best make a rough and imperfect approximation of adequacy—that reality refuses cognitive domestication, so that our best cognitive efforts represent a valiant but never totally satisfactory attempt to "get it right." Such a position is not a radical scepticism that denies the availability of any and all useful information about reality, but a mitigated scepticism that insists that thought at best affords rough information about reality—not by way of definitive and indefeasible *epistémê*, but by way of a "rational belief" that is inevitably imperfect and defective (its rationality notwithstanding). An element of tentativeness should always attend our philosophical theories—we can never rest assured that they will not need to be revamped and shored up by our successors (quite to the contrary, we can count on it!).

As this line of thought indicates, two basic goals set the scene for philosophical inquiry: (i) the urge to know, to secure answers to our questions, to enhance our cognitive resources, to enlarge our information, to extend the range of accepted theses, to fill up an intellectual vacuum. But this in the nature of the case—given the character of its "data"—inexorably leads to over-commitment, to informational overcrowding to inconsistency, and now comes (ii), the urge to rationality: to have a coherent theory, to keep our commitments consistent and harmoniously coordinated. The first impetus is expansive and ampliative, the second contractive and eliminative. Both point in the direction of systematization, with its characteristic concern for comprehensiveness and harmonization.

Philosophy as Truth Estimation

As a venture in rational inquiry, philosophy seeks for the best available, the "rationally optimal," answers to our information-in-hand-transcending questions about how matters stand in the world. And experience-based conjecture—theorizing, if you will—is the most promising available instrument for question resolution in the face of imperfect information. It is a tool for use by finite intelligences, providing them not with the best *possible* answer (in some rarified sense of this term), but with the best *available* answer, the putative best that one can manage to secure in the actually existing conditions in which we do and must conduct our epistemic labors.

In philosophy, as elsewhere throughout the domain of estimation, one confronts an inevitable risk of error. This risk takes two forms. On the one hand, we face errors of commission in possibly accepting what is false. On the other hand, we face errors of omission by failing to accept what is true. Like any other cognitive enterprise, philosophy has to navigate the difficult passage between ignorance and mistakes.

Two equally unacceptable extremes offer themselves at this stage. That first is to accept nothing, to fall into pervasive scepticism. Here we achieve a total exemption from errors of commission—but unfortunately do so at the expense of endless errors of omission. The other extreme is to fall into pervasive gullibility, to accept pretty much everything that is put before us. Here we achieve a total exemption from errors of omission—but unfortunately do so at the expense of maximal errors of commission. In philosophy, as in other branches of rational inquiry, we must strive for the best available middle way—the best available balance. Though we realize that there are no guarantees, we do desire and require reasonable estimates.

The need for such an estimative approach is easy to see. After all, we .... in a world not of our making where we have to do the best we can with the limited means at our disposal. We must recognize that there is no prospect of assessing the truth—or presumptive truth—of claims (be they philosophical or scientific) independently of the use of our imperfect mechanisms of inquiry and systematization. And here it is *estimation* that affords the best means for doing the job. We are not—and presumably will never be—in a position to stake totally secure claims to the definitive truth regarding those great issues of philosophical interest. But we certainly can—and indeed must—do the best we can to achieve a reasonable *estimate* of the truth. We can and do *aim* at the truth in our inquiries, even in circumstances where we cannot make foolproof pretensions to its attainment, and where we have no alternative but to settle for the *best available estimate* of the truth of the matter—that estimate for which the best case can be made, according to the appropriate standards of rational cogency.

Yet despite those guarding qualifications about feasibility and practicability, the "best available" answer at issue here is intended in a rather strong sense. We want not just an "answer" of some sort, but a viable and acceptable answer—one whose tenability we are willing to commit ourselves to. The rational conjecture at issue is not to be a product of *mere guesswork*, but one of *responsible estimation* in a strict sense of the term. It is not *just* an estimate of the true answer that we want, but an estimate that is sensible and defensible: *tenable*, in short. We may need to resort to more information than is actually given, but we do not want to make it up "out of thin air." The provision of reasonable warrant for rational assurance is the object of the enterprise. Rational inquiry is a matter of doing no more—but also no less—than the best we can manage to realize in its prevailing epistemic circumstances. Nevertheless, the fact remains that the rationally indicated answer does in fact afford our most promising estimate of the true answer—that for whose acceptance as true the optimal overall case be constructed in the circumstances at hand.

Now with regard to those "big issues" that constitute the agenda of philosophy, the systematization of otherwise available information is the best policy. And systematization in the context of the available background information is nothing other than the process for making out this rationally best case. It is thus rational conjecture as based on and emerging from systematic considerations that is the key method of philosophical inquiry, affording our best hope for obtaining cogent answers to the questions that confront us in this domain. Let us consider more closely just what is involved here.

The Data of Philosophy

In philosophizing we strive for rational coherence in achieving answers to our questions. But how is one to proceed in this venture? It is clear that here, as in other branches of inquiry, we begin with data.

Neither individually nor collectively do we humans begin our cognitive quest empty handed, equipped with only a blank tablet. Be it as single individuals or as entire generations, we always begin with a diversified cognitive heritage, falling heir to the great mass of information and misinformation of our predecessors—one must extend it. What William James called our "funded experience" of the world's ways—of its nature and our place within it—constitute the *data* at philosophy's disposal in its endeavor to accomplish its question-resolving work. These specifically include:

- Common-sense beliefs, common knowledge, and what have been "the ordinary convictions of the plain man" since time immemorial;

- The facts (or purported facts) afforded by the science of the day; the views of well-informed "experts" and "authorities";

- The lessons we derive from our dealings with the world in everyday life;

- The received opinions that constitute the worldview of the day; views that accord with the "spirit of the times" and the ambient convictions of one's cultural context;
- Tradition, inherited lore, and ancestral wisdom (including religious tradition);
- The "teachings of history," as best we can discern them.

There is no clear limit to the scope of philosophy's potentially useful data. The lessons of human experience in all of its cognitive dimensions afford the materials of philosophy. No plausible source of information about how matters stand [...] [...] fails to bring grist to the mill. The whole range of the (purportedly) established "facts of experience" furnishes the extra-philosophical inputs for our philosophizing—the potentially usable materials, as it were, for our philosophical reflections.

And all of these data have much to be said for them: common sense, tradition, general belief, and plausible prior theorizing—the sum total of the different sectors of "our experience." They all merit consideration: all exert some degree of cognitive pressure in having a claim upon us. Yet, while those data deserve respect, they do not deserve acceptance. And they certainly do not constitute established knowledge. There is nothing sacred and sacrosanct about them. For, taken as a whole, the data are too much for tenability—collectively they generally run into conflicts and contradictions. The long and short of it is that the data of philosophy constitute a plethora of fact (or purported fact) so ample as to threaten to sink any ship that carries so heavy a cargo. The constraint they put upon us is thus not peremptory and absolute—they do not represent certainties to which we must cling to at all costs. Even the plainest of "plain facts" can be questioned, as indeed some of them must be, since in the aggregate they are collectively inconsistent.

And this is the condition of philosophy's data in general. For the philosopher, nothing is absolutely sacred. The difficulty is—and always has been—that the data of philosophy afford an embarrassment of riches. They engender a situation of cognitive over-commitment within which inconsistencies arise. For they are not only manifold and diversified but invariably yield discordant results. Taken altogether in their grand totality, the data are inconsistent. And here philosophy finds its work cut out for it.

In philosophy, we cannot accept all those "givens" as certified facts that must be endorsed wholly and unqualifiedly. Every datum is defeasible. Anything might, in the final analysis, have to be abandoned, whatever its source: science, common sense, common knowledge, the whole lot. Those data are not truths but only plausibilities. Nothing about them is immune to criticism and possible rejection; everything is potentially at risk. One recent theorist quips: "No philosophical, or any other, theory can provide a view which violates common sense and remain logically consistent. For the truth of common sense is assumed by all theories. . . . This necessity to conform to common sense establishes a constraint upon the interpretations philosophical theories can offer."[7] But this is very problematic. The landscape of philosophical history is littered with theories that tread common sense underfoot. There are no sacred cows in philosophy—common sense least of all. As philosophy goes about its work of rendering our beliefs coherent, something to which we are deeply attached will have to give, and we can never say at the outset where the blow will or will not fall. Systemic considerations may in the end lead to difficulties at any point.

For these data do indeed all have some degree of merit and, given our cognitive situation, it would be very convenient if they turned out to be true. Philosophy cannot simply turn its back on these data without further ado. Its methodology must be one of damage control and salvage. For as regards those data, it should always be our goal to save as much as we coherently can.

Metaphilosophical Issues

To this point, the tenor of the discussion has been to offer a series of assertions along the lines of: this is what philosophy is; this is what philosophy does; this is how philosophizing works. But what justifies this way of talking? What reason is there to think that matters indeed stand as claimed?

This is a question that can, in the final analysis, be answered only *genetically*, by linking the response to and duly coordinating it with the historical facts about how philosophizing has actually been carried on over the years. What philosophy is all about is not writ large in the lineaments of theory, but it is something that must be gleaned from the inspectable realities of philosophical practice. And so, while the history of physics may be largely irrelevant for physicists, the history of philosophy is unavoidably relevant for philosophers. What philosophers *should* do has to emerge from a critical analysis of what philosophers *have been* doing. The history of philosophy is not a part of philosophy, but philosophy cannot get on without it.

All the same, it is lamentable that now, more than two hundred years later, there are still philosophers whose modus operandi invites Kant's classic complaint (at the start of the introduction of the *Prolegomena*) that "there are scholarly men for whom the history of philosophy (both ancient and modern) is philosophy itself." For the fact is that philosophy and history of philosophy *address different questions*—in the former instance, what is the case about an issue, and in the latter, what someone, X, thought to be the case. To address the former question we must speak on our own account. A philosopher cannot be a commission agent trading in the doctrines of others; in the final analysis he or she must deal on his or her own account. There must be a shift from "X thinks that A is the answer to the question Q" to the position that we ourselves are prepared to endorse for substantively cogent reasons. No amount of exposition and clarification regarding the thought of X and of Y will themselves answer the question on our agenda. To do so, we must decide not what people thought or meant but what is correct with respect to the issues. And so while the history of philosophy is indeed an indispensable instrument of philosophy—in a science of concepts, ideas, problems, issues, theories, and so on—these are no more than *data* for our philosophizing. Actually to philosophize we must do more than note and consolidate such data, we must appraise and evaluate them on our own account. Philosophers must speak for themselves and conduct their business on their own account. They cannot hide themselves behind what X thinks or what Y thinks, but must in the end present a position of their own with respect to *what is to be thought*. The history of philosophy is not—and cannot be—a substitute for philosophy itself.

Nevertheless, the fact is that metaphilosophy—the study of the nature and methodology of the discipline—is also an integral component of philosophy. Unlike the situation with chemistry or with physiology, questions about the nature of philosophy belong to the discipline itself. And so, these questions about methodology cannot really be resolved by recourse to some sort of philosophy-neutral methodology. Only at the end of the day—only when we have pursued our philosophical inquiries to an adequate stage of development—will it become possible to see, with the wisdom of a more synoptic hindsight, as it were, that the selection of a methodological starting point was in fact proper and appropriate. It is part and parcel of the coherentist nature of philosophical method that our analysis must issue in smoothly self-supportive cycles and climates. Circularity in philosophical argumentation is not necessarily vicious. On the contrary, it can and should exhibit the ultimately self-sustaining nature of rational inquiry at large. Herein lies a key part of the reason why philosophy must be developed systematically—that is, as a system.

If you cannot fit your philosophical contentions into a smooth systemic unison with what you otherwise know then there is something seriously amiss with them. To be sure, this does not mean that the discussion will not, here and there, be projected into contentions that are controversial and seemingly eccentric. For sometimes the best reason for adopting a controversial and apparently strange thesis is that it contributes significantly to the systemic coordination of the familiar by serving to unify and rationalize a mass of material, much of which seems comparatively unproblematic. For example, our basic thesis that philosophy exists to make sense of the things we know is far from being a philosophical truism. But that does not preclude its ultimate appropriations.

The cardinal task of philosophy is thus to impart systemic order into the domain of relevant data; to render them consistent, compatible, and smoothly coordinated. Its commitment to instilling harmonious coherence into the manifold of our putative knowledge means that systematization is the prime and principal instrument of philosophical methodology. One might, in fact, define philosophy as the rational systematization of our thoughts on basic issues—the "basic principles" of our understanding of the world and our place within it. We become involved in philosophy in our endeavor to make systemic sense of the extraphilosophical "facts"—when we try to answer those big questions by systematizing what we think we know about the world, pushing our "knowledge" to its ultimate conclusions, and combining items usually kept in convenient separation. Philosophy is the policeman of thought, as it were, the agent for maintaining law and order in our cognitive endeavors.

2

Knowledge and Scepticism

The Sceptic's "No Certainty" Argument

Claims to knowledge do not admit of qualification by any element of doubt or cavil: authentic knowledge is only that which is certain and undeniably true. It makes no sense to say "*X* knows that _____, but it may possibly not be so." If there were any questions about it we could have to say "*X thinks* he knows that _____" instead of the unqualified "*X* knows that _____."

But do we ever achieve absolute certainty? Perhaps sometimes in matters relating to oneself—as per Descartes' example, "I am thinking." But surely impersonal matters of objective fact are in a more difficult position.

On this basis, philosophers since Plato's[1] day have stressed the unattainability of absolutes in our knowledge regarding this world. And a straightforward and plausible argument for scepticism is at work here. If a contention is to be absolutely secure relative to the grounds by which it is supported, then its content must not go beyond the content of those contentions that serve as grounds for the claim.

But with claims of objective fact there is always an "evidential gap," because of the data at our disposal we exhaust the content of such claims. "The apple *looks red* to me" is an autobiographical statement about me, while "The apple *is red*" is an objective claim that has involvements (for example, how it will look to others in different sorts of light) that I have not checked and cannot check in toto. Factual claims are invariably such that there is a wide gap between the evidence we need to have at our disposal to make a warranted claim and the content of this claim. The milkman leaves the familiar sort of bottle of white liquid on the doorstep. One does not hesitate to call it "milk." A small cylinder of hard, white, earthen material is lying next to the blackboard. One does not hesitate to call it "chalk." The content of such claims clearly ranges far wider than our meager evidence and extends to chemical composition, sources of origin, behavior under pressure, and so on and so forth. And this story is a standard one. For the fact is that all of our statements regarding matters of objective fact (that is, "That is an apple" as opposed to "Something appears to me to be an apple") are such that the content of the claim—its overall set of commitments and implications—moves far beyond the (relatively meager) evidence for it that is actually at our disposal. And this evidential gap between the evidence in hand and the substantive contention at issue seemingly foredooms any prospect of attaining certainty.[2] To all intents and purposes, this circumstance squarely violates the absolutism of claims to knowledge. What we have called "the facts of cognitive life" are to all appearances such that the definitive conditions for knowledge cannot be met in the factual domain. This, at any rate, is the sceptic's contention.

The sceptic bolsters cognitive nihilism by inserting into the evidential gap the sharp wedge of a knowledge-defeating possibility—the supposition that life is but a dream, or the hypothesis of the Cartesian archdeceiver and its latter-day successor, the wicked, powerful scientist. The unattainability of any knowledge in matters of objective fact is advanced by the sceptic on the basis of the impossibility in principle of ruling out such certainty-defeating possibilities. Do we, for example, really *know for sure* that the person who jumps off the Empire State Building will crash downwards? Why should they not float gently skywards? This would, no doubt, surprise us, but surprises do happen; in such matters of generalization "we may be in no better position than the chicken which unexpectedly has its neck wrung."[3] After all, the sceptic insists that we are caught in the uncomfortable grip of the "No Certainty" Argument:[4]

1. All knowledge-claims are committed to a demand for absolute certainty.

2. Objective factual claims are always evidence-transcending: they are never in a position to meet absolutistic demands. Our objective factual claims can never amount to actual *knowledge*.[5]

The task of these present deliberations is to examine whether—and how—this sort of sceptical argumentation can be defeated.[6]

The Role of Certainty

Scepticism's insistence to the contrary notwithstanding, a claim's being absolutely certain—or even *being* true—in fact just is not a necessary precondition for staking a rationally warranted *claim* to knowledge. Consider the two propositions:

- *P* is justifiably held by *X* to be true.
- *P* is true.

Does the first entail or presuppose the second? Surely not. For the evidence in hand that suffices to justify someone in holding a thesis to be true need not provide a deductive guarantee of this thesis. A strictly analogous situation is presented with the pair:

- *P* is justifiably held by *X* to be certain.
- *P* is certain.

Again, the first proposition does not entail or require the second. The standard gap between the epistemic issue of what someone justifiably holds to be and the ontological issue of what is again comes into the picture. One must be willing to admit in general the existence of a gap between warranted assertability and ultimate correctness, holding that on occasion even incorrect theses can be maintained with due warrant. And there is no decisive reason for blocking the application of this general rule to certainty-claims in particular. It

stand up in the final analysis to the challenges of a difficult and often recalcitrant world. No assurances that extend beyond the limits of the possible can be given—or sensibly asked for.

It is thus needful to speak of a contrast between "the hyperbolic certainty of the philosopher" and "the mundane certainty of the plain man" in the setting of the actual transaction of our cognitive business.[9] Philosophers have often felt driven to a conception of knowledge so rigid as to yield the result that there is little if anything left that one can ever be said to know. Indeed, sceptical thinkers of this inclination launch upon an explication of the "nature of knowledge" that sets the standards of its attainment so high that it becomes, in principle, impossible for anything to meet such hyperbolic demands. Against this tendency, it is proper to insist that while what is known must indeed be true—and certainly true—it is nevertheless in order to insist that the conceptions at issue can and should be so construed that there are realistic and realizable circumstances in which our claims to *certainty* and to *knowledge* are perfectly legitimate and altogether justified. A doctrine that admits the defeasibility of quite appropriate claims to knowledge need involve no contradictions in terms.

Pragmatic Inconsistency

The difference between real and merely conjectural possibilities of error is crucial for rational warrant for claims or concessions to knowledge. A real possibility must be case-specific and not abstractly generic and somehow based on general principles alone. And this, it must be insisted, is not incompatible with the existence of a "purely theoretical" (let alone "purely logical") prospect of error. There is thus no real anomaly in holding on the one hand that knowledge "must be certain" (in the *effective* sense of this term) and on the other hand that a valid knowledge claim "might possibly be wrong" (with "might" construed in the light of a merely theoretical or "purely logical" mode of possibility).

For example, we need not in the usual course of things exert ourselves in an endeavor to rule out the imaginative sceptic's demonology of uncannily real dreams, deceitful demons, powerful evil scientists, and so forth. The general principles and presumptions of the domain suffice to put all this aside. To claim knowledge in specific cases, all we need to do is eliminate those case-specific considerations that would countervail against the claim at issue in a realistic and plausible way.

If we sometimes fall into error even when doing the best we can, how can we tell that we have not done so in the present case? And if we cannot *guarantee* truth, then how can we speak of *knowledge*?

The answer is simple. If we have done all that can reasonably be asked of us, the best that can realistically be done, then there can be no need for any *further* assurance. The objection suggests that we must be in a position to do better than the best we can. And this is of course absurd—and therefore cannot and must not be asked of us.

Accordingly, the "No Certainty" Argument becomes invalidated. It is not true that knowledge claims are committed to a demand for absolute certainty in any hyperbolically inaccessible way. They are indeed committed to a demand for certainty, but this "certainty" must be construed realistically—in the effective, mundane, and practical sense of the term. The certainty at issue in our knowledge-claims is not inherently unattainable; it is simply that the grounding in hand must be strong enough to indicate that further substantiation is superfluous in the sense of yielding every reasonable assurance that the thing at issue is as certain as something of its sort need appropriately be. To repeat: it suffices to ask for an adequate grounding for these claims; a logically exhaustive grounding is not a reasonable requirement, for the simple reason—so eloquently stressed by the sceptic himself—that it is in principle incapable of being satisfied.

The sceptic sets up standards upon "knowledge" that are so unrealistic as to move outside the range of considerations at work in the conception as it actually functions in the language. He insists upon construing knowledge in such a way as to foist upon the cognitivist a Sisyphus-like task by subjecting all knowledge-claims to an effectively undischargeable burden of proof. But this hyperbolic standard separates the sceptic from the concept of knowledge as it functions in common life and in (most) philosophical discussions.

Clearly, if it is *knowledge* as the language deals with it that we propose to discuss—and not some artificial construct whose consideration constitutes a change of subject—then we must abide by the ground rules of the conceptual scheme that is at issue. And this simply is not a negotiable matter of playing the game by X's rules instead of Y's. It is not a conventional game that is defined by the rules we arbitrarily adopt, but an impersonal set of rules established in the public instrumentality of a language. We must not afford the sceptic the luxury of a permission to rewrite, at his or her own whim, the warranting standards for the terminology of our cognitive discourse.

The sceptic simply is not free to impose hyperbolic probative standards upon us. If sceptics wish to dispute about knowledge, they must take the concept as they find it in the language-based conceptual system that we actually use. (They cannot substitute a more rigoristic standard for counting as knowledge, any more than they can substitute a more rigoristic standard for counting as a dog, say a standard that ruled Chihuahuas out as just too small.) In failing to make effective contact with the conceptual scheme in which our actual knowledge-claims in fact function, the sceptic assumes an irrational posture in the debate. And the crucial fact is that our actual standards here are rooted in the ground rules for rational controversy and the conditions for making out a conclusive (probatively solid) case, ground rules and conditions in which all of the standard mechanisms of presumptions and burden of proof are embedded.

Scepticism and Risk

The scientific researcher, the inquiring philosopher, and the plain human all desire and strive for information about the "real" world. The sceptic rejects their ventures as vain and their hopes as foredoomed to disappointment from the very outset. As the sceptic sees it, any and all sufficiently trustworthy information about factual matters is simply unavailable as a matter of general principle. To put such a radical scepticism into a sensible perspective, it is useful to consider the issue of cognitive rationality in the light of the situation of risk taking in general.

There are three very different sorts of personal approaches to risk and three very different sorts of personalities corresponding to these approaches, as follows:

Type 1: *Risk avoiders*

Type 2: *Risk calculators*

   Type 2.1: *Cautious*

   Type 2.2: *Daring*

Type 3: *Risk seekers*

The type 1, risk-avoidance approach calls for risk aversion and evasion. Its adherents have little or no tolerance for risk and gambling. Their approach to risk is altogether negative. Their mottos are: take no chances, always expect the worst, and play it safe.

The type 2, risk-calculating approach to risk is more realistic. It is a guarded middle-of-the-road position, based on due care and calculation. It comes in two varieties. The type 2.1, cautiously-calculating approach sees risk taking as subject to a negative presumption, which can, however, be defeated by suitably large benefits. Its line is: avoid risks unless it is relatively clear that a suitably large gain beckons at sufficiently suspicious odds. It reflects the path of prudence and guarded caution. The type 2.2, daringly-calculating approach sees risk taking as subject to a positive presumption, which can, however, be defeated by suitably large negativities. Its line is: be prepared to take risks unless it is relatively clear that an unacceptably large loss threatens at sufficiently inauspicious odds. It reflects the path of optimistic hopefulness.

The type 3, risk-seeking approach sees risk as something to be welcomed and courted. Its adherents close their eyes to danger and take a rosy view of risky situations. The mind of the risk seeker is intent on the delightful situation of a favorable issue of events: the sweet savor of success is already in his nostrils. Risk seekers are chance takers and go-for-broke gamblers. They react to risk the way an old warhorse responds to the sound of the musketry: with eager anticipation and positive relish. Their motto is: things will work out.

In the conduct of practical affairs, risk avoiders are hypercautious; they have no stomach for uncertainty and insist on playing it absolutely safe. In any potentially unfavorable situation, the mind of the risk avoider is given to imagining the myriad things that could go wrong. Risk seekers, on the other hand, leap first and look later, apparently counting on a benign fate to ensure that all will be well; they dwell in the heady atmosphere of "anything may happen." Risk calculators take a middle-of-the-road approach. Proceeding with care, they take due safeguards but still run risks when the situation looks sufficiently favorable. It is thus clear that people can have very different attitudes toward risk.

The situation with regard to specifically cognitive risks can be approached as simply a special case of the general strategies sketched above. In particular, it is clear that risk avoidance stands coordinate with scepticism. The sceptic's line is: run no risk of error; take no chances; accept nothing that does not come with ironclad guarantees. And the proviso here is largely academic, seeing that little if anything in this world comes with ironclad guarantees—certainly nothing by way of interesting knowledge. By contrast, the adventuresome syncretist is inclined to think that anything goes. His cognitive stance is tolerant and open to input from all quarters. He is gullible, as it were, and stands ready to endorse everything and to see good on all sides. The evidentialist, on the other hand, conducts his cognitive business with comparative care and calculation, regarding various sorts of claims as perfectly acceptable, provided that the evidential circumstances are duly favorable.

Turning now to the specifically cognitive case, it may be observed that the sceptic succeeds splendidly in averting misfortunes of the second kind. He makes no errors of commission; by accepting nothing, he accepts nothing false. But, of course, he loses out on the opportunity to obtain any sort of information. The sceptic thus errs on the side of safety, even as the syncretist errs on that of gullibility. The sensible course is clearly that of a prudent calculation of risks.

The sceptic accepts nothing, the evidentialist only the chosen few, the syncretist virtually anything. In effect, the positions at issue in scepticism, syncretism, and evidentialism simply replicate, in the specifically cognitive domain, the various approaches to risks at large. It must, however, be recognized that in general two fundamentally different kinds of misfortunes are possible in situations where risks are run and chances taken:

1. We reject something that, as it turns out, we should have accepted. We decline to take the chance, we avoid running the

risk at issue, but things turn out favorably after all, so that we lose out on the gamble.

2. We accept something that, as it turns out, we should have rejected. We do take the chance and run the risk at issue, but things go wrong, so that we lose the gamble.

If we are risk seekers, we will incur few misfortunes of the first kind, but, things being what they are, many of the second kind will befall us. On the other hand, if we are risk avoiders, we shall suffer few misfortunes of the second kind, but shall inevitably incur many of the first. The overall situation has the general structure depicted in display 2.1.

Clearly, the reasonable thing to do is to adopt a policy that minimizes misfortunes overall. It is thus evident that both type 1 and type 3 approaches will, in general, fail to be rationally optimal. Both approaches engender too many misfortunes for comfort. The sensible and prudent thing is to adopt the middle-of-the-road policy of

Display 2.1. Risk Acceptance and Misfortunes

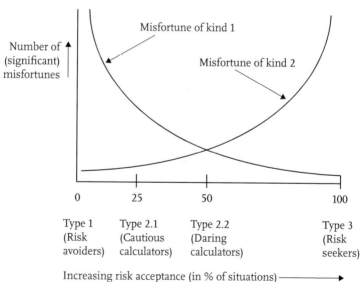

Number of (significant) misfortunes

Misfortune of kind 1

Misfortune of kind 2

0	25	50	100
Type 1 (Risk avoiders)	Type 2.1 (Cautious calculators)	Type 2.2 (Daring calculators)	Type 3 (Risk seekers)

Increasing risk acceptance (in % of situations) ⟶

risk calculation, striving as best we can to balance the positive risks of outright loss against the negative ones of lost opportunity. Rationality thus contraindicates approaches of type 1 and type 2, taking the line of the counsel: neither avoid nor court risks but manage them prudently in the search for an overall minimization of misfortunes. The rule of reason calls for sensible management and a prudent calculation of risks; it standardly enjoins upon us the Aristotelian golden mean between the extremes of risk avoidance and risk seeking.

Being mistaken is unquestionably a negativity. When we accept something false, we have failed in our endeavors to get a clear view of things—to answer our questions correctly. And moreover, mistakes tend to ramify, to infect environing issues. If I (correctly) realize that P logically entails a, but incorrectly believe not-a, then I am constrained to accept not-P, which may well be quite wrong. Error is fertile of further error. So quite apart from practical matters (suffering painful practical consequences when things go wrong), there are also the purely cognitive penalties of mistakes—entrapment in an incorrect view of things. All this must be granted and taken into account. But the fact remains that errors of commission are not the only sorts of misfortune there are.[10] Ignorance, lack of information, cognitive disconnection from the world's course of things—in short, errors of omission—are also negativities of substantial proportions. This too is something we must work into our reckoning.

In claiming that their position wins out because it avoids mistakes, sceptics use a fallacious system of scoring. While they indeed make the fewest errors of one kind, it is at the cost of proliferating those of another kind. Once we look on this matter of error realistically, the sceptic's vaunted advantage vanishes. The sceptic is simply a risk avoider, who is prepared to take no risks and who stubbornly insists on minimizing errors of the second kind alone, heedless of falling into errors of the first kind at every opportunity.

Ultimately, we face a question of value trade-offs. Are we prepared to run a greater risk of mistakes to secure the potential benefit of an enlarged understanding? In the end, the matter is one of priorities and values—safety versus information, ontological economy versus cognitive advantage, epistemological risk aversion versus the impetus to understanding—weighing the negativity of ignorance and incomprehension against the risk of mistakes and misinformation.

The Deficiency of Scepticism

The sceptic too readily loses sight of the purposes of our cognitive endeavors. The object of rational inquiry is not just to avoid error but to answer our questions, to secure *information* about the world. And here, as elsewhere, "nothing ventured, nothing gained" is the operative principle. Granted, a systematic abstention from cognitive involvement is a surefire safeguard against one kind of error. But, it affords this security at too steep a price. The shortcoming of that "no risk" option is that it guarantees failure from the very outset.

It is self-defeating to follow the radical sceptic into letting discretion be the whole of epistemic valor by systematically avoiding the acceptance of anything whatsoever in the domain of empirical fact. To be sure, when we set out to acquire information we may well discover in the end that, try as we will, success in reaching our goal is beyond our means. But we shall *certainly* get nowhere at all if we do not even set out on the journey—which is exactly what the sceptic's blanket proscription of acceptance amounts to.

In "playing the game" of making assertions and laying claims to credence, we may well lose: our contentions may turn out to be mistaken. But, in a refusal to play this game at all, we face not just the possibility but the certainty of losing the prize—we abandon any chance to realize our cognitive objectives. A sceptical policy of systematic avoidance of acceptance is fundamentally *irrational*, because it blocks from the very outset any prospect of realizing the inherent goals of the enterprise of factual inquiry. In cognition, as in other sectors of life, there are no guarantees, no ways of averting risk altogether, no option that is totally safe and secure. The best and most we can do is to make optimal use of the resources at our disposal, to "manage" risks as best we can. To decline to do this by refusing to accept any sort of risk is to become immobilized. The sceptic thus pays a great price for the comfort of safety and security. If we want information—if we deem ignorance no less a negativity than error—then we must be prepared to "take the gamble" of answering our questions in ways that risk some possibility of error. A middle-of-the-road evidentialism emerges as the most sensible approach.

To be sure, the sceptical challenge to the project of empirical inquiry based on principles of cognitive rationality has a very plausible look about it. Our means for the acquisition of factual knowledge are unquestionably imperfect. Where, for example, are the "scientific truths" of yesteryear—those earth-shaking syntheses of Aristotle and Ptolemy, of Newton and Maxwell? Virtually no part of them has survived wholly unscathed. And given this past course of bitter experience, how can we possibly validate our *present* acceptance of factual contentions in a rationally convincing way?

Against this background, the sceptic *seemingly* moves within the orbit of rationality. But only seemingly so. Perhaps, no other objection to radical scepticism in the factual domain is as impressive as the fact that, for the all-out sceptic, any and all assertions about the world's objective facts must lie on the same cognitive plane. No contention—no matter how bizarre—is any better off than any other in point of its legitimate credentials. For the thoroughgoing sceptic there just is no rationally relevant difference between "more than three people are currently living in China" and "there are at present fewer than three automobiles in North America." As far as the cognitive venture goes, it stands committed to the view that there is "nothing to choose" in point of warrant between one factual claim and another. Radical scepticism is an H-bomb that levels everything in the cognitive domain.

The all-out septic writes off at the very outset a prospect whose abandonment would only be rationally defensible at the very end. As Charles Sanders Peirce never tired of maintaining, inquiry only has a point if we accept from the outset that there is some prospect that it may terminate in a satisfactory answer to our questions. He indicated the appropriate stance with trenchant cogency: "The first question, then, which I have to ask is: Supposing such a thing to be true, what is the kind of proof which I ought to demand to satisfy me of its truth?"[11] A general epistemic policy that would, as a matter of principle, make it impossible for us to discover something that is ex hypothesi the case is clearly irrational. And the sceptical proscription of all acceptance is obviously such a policy—one that abrogates the project of inquiry at the very outset, without according it the benefit of a fair trial. A presumption in favor of rationality—cognitive rationality included—is rationally inescapable. It could, to be sure, eventuate at the end of the day that satisfactory knowledge of physical reality is unachievable. But, until the proverbial end of the day arrives, we can and should proceed with the idea that this possibility is not in prospect. "Never bar the path of inquiry," Peirce rightly insisted. And radical scepticism's fatal flaw is that it aborts inquiry at the start.

As Aristotle sagely observed, "Man by nature desires to know." In this cognitive sphere, reason cannot leave well enough alone, but insists upon a continual enhancement in the range and depth of our understanding of ourselves and of the world about us. Cognitive rationality is a matter of using cogent reasons to govern one's acceptance of beliefs—of answering one's questions in the best feasible way. But is this project realizable at all? We must consider the sceptic's long-standing challenge that it is not. For, the sceptic—in his more radical moments, at any rate—insists that there is never a satisfactory justification for accepting anything whatsoever. By rejecting the very possibility of securing trustworthy information in factual matters, scepticism sets up a purportedly decisive obstacle to implementing these aims of reason.

Philosophical sceptics generally set up some abstract standard of absolutistic certainty and then try to show that no knowledge claims in a certain area (sense, memory, scientific theory, and the like) can possibly meet the conditions of this standard. From this circumstance, the impossibility of such a category of "knowledge" is accordingly inferred. But this inference is totally misguided. For what follows is rather the inappropriateness or incorrectness of the standard at issue. If the vaunted standard is such that knowledge claims cannot possibly meet it, the moral is not "too bad for knowledge claims," but "too bad for the standard." Any position that precludes in principle the possibility of valid knowledge claims thereby effectively manifests its own unacceptability.

The sceptic's argument is a double-edged sword that cuts both ways and inflicts the more serious damage upon itself. It is senseless to impose on something qualification conditions that it cannot in the very nature of things meet. After all, it simply makes no sense to require us to do more than the best that is possible in any situation—cognition included. But rationality also conveys the comforting realization that more than this cannot be required of us: we are clearly entitled to see the best that can be done as good enough.

Scepticism surrenders from the very start any prospect of realizing our cognitive purposes and aspirations. And on this basis, it runs counter to the teleological enterprise to which we humans stand committed to in virtue of being the sort of intelligent creatures we are. It is ultimately this collision between scepticism and our need for the products of rational inquiry that makes the rejection of scepticism a rational imperative.[12]

3

Limits of Science

Conditions of Perfected Science

How far can the scientific enterprise advance toward a definitive understanding of reality? Might science attain a point of recognizable completion? Is the achievement of perfected science a genuine possibility, even in theory when all of the "merely practical" obstacles are put aside as somehow incidental?

What would *perfected science* actually be like? What sort of standards would it have to meet? Clearly, it would have to complete in full the discharge of natural science's mandate or mission. Now, the goal-structure of scientific inquiry covers a good deal of ground. It is diversified and complex, spreading across both the cognitive/theoretical and active/practical sectors. It encompasses the traditional quartet of description, explanation, prediction, and control, in line with display 3.1.

The theoretical sector of science concerns itself with matters of characterizing, explaining, accounting for, and rendering intelligible—with purely intellectual and informative issues, in short.

Display 3.1. Goal-Structure of Scientific Inquiry

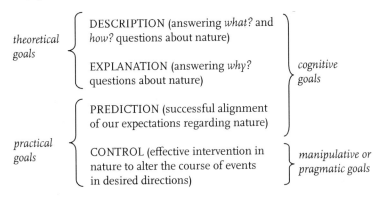

By contrast, the practical sector is concerned with deciding actions, guiding expectations, and, in general, with achieving the control over our environment that is required for the satisfactory conduct of our affairs. The former sector thus deals with what science enables us to *say*, and the latter with what it enables us to *do*. The one relates to our role as spectators of nature, the other to our role as active participants.

It thus appears that if we are to claim that our science has attained a perfected condition, it would have to satisfy (at least) the four following conditions:

1. *Erotetic completeness*: It must answer, in principle at any rate, all those descriptive and explanatory questions that it countenances as legitimately raisable and must accordingly explain everything it deems explicable.

2. *Predictive completeness*: It must provide the cognitive basis for accurately predicting those eventuations that are in principle predictable (that is, those that it recognizes as such).

3. *Pragmatic completeness*: It must provide the requisite cognitive means for doing whatever is feasible for beings like ourselves to do in the circumstances in which we labor.

4. *Temporal finality* (the omega-condition of ultimate finality): It must leave no room for expecting further substantial changes that destabilize the existing state of scientific knowledge.

Each of these modes of substantive completeness deserves detailed consideration. First, however, one brief preliminary remark: it is clear that any condition of science that might qualify as "perfected" would have to meet certain formal requirements of systemic unity. If, for example, there are different routes to one and the same question (for instance, if both astronomy and geology can inform us about the age of the Earth), then these answers will certainly have to be consistent. Perfected science will have to meet certain requirements of structural systematicity in the manner of its articulation: it must be coherent, consistent, consonant, uniform, harmonious, and so on. Such requirements represent purely formal cognitive demands upon the architectonic of articulation of a body of science that could lay any claim to perfection. Interesting and important though they are, we shall not, however, trouble about these *formal* requirements here, our present concern being with various *substantive* issues.[1]

Issues of Theoretical Completeness

Erotetic completeness is surely an unattainable mirage. We can never exhaust the possibility of questions. The Kantian principle of question propagation means that inquiry—the dialectic of questions and answers—can never get to the ultimate bottom of things.

Any adequate theory of inquiry must recognize that the ongoing progress of science is a process of *conceptual* innovation that always leaves certain theses wholly outside the cognitive range of the inquirers of any particular period. This means that there will always be facts (or plausible candidate facts) about a thing that we do not *know*, because we cannot even conceive of them. For to grasp such a fact calls for taking a perspective of consideration that we simply do not have, since the state of our knowledge (or purported knowledge) has not yet advanced to a point at which its entertainment is feasible. In bringing conceptual innovation about, cognitive progress makes it possible to consider new possibilities that were heretofore conceptually inaccessible.

After all, could we ever actually achieve erotetic completeness (Q-completeness)—the condition of being able to resolve, in principle, all of our (legitimately posable) questions about the world? Could we ever find ourselves in this position?[2] In theory, yes. A body of science certainly could be such as to provide answers to all those questions it allows to arise. But just how meaningful would this mode of completeness be?

It is sobering to realize that the erotetic completeness of a state of science, S, does not necessarily betoken its comprehensiveness or sufficiency. It might reflect the paucity of the range of questions we are prepared to contemplate—a deficiency of imagination, so to speak. When the range of our knowledge is sufficiently restricted, then its Q-completeness will merely reflect this impoverishment rather than its intrinsic adequacy. Conceivably, if improbably, science might reach a purely fortuitous equilibrium between problems and solutions. It could eventually be "completed" in the narrow erotetic sense—providing an answer to every question one can raise in the then-existing (albeit still imperfect) state of knowledge—without thereby being completed in the larger sense of answering the questions that would arise if only one could probe nature just a bit more deeply. And so, our corpus of scientific knowledge could be erotetically complete and yet fundamentally inadequate. Thus, even if realized, this erotetic mode of completeness would not be particularly meaningful. (To be sure, this discussion proceeds at the level of supposition contrary to fact. The exfoliation of new questions from old in the course of scientific inquiry that is at issue in Kant's principle of question-propagation spells the infeasibility of ever attaining Q-completeness.)

The preceding considerations illustrate a more general circumstance. Any claim to the realization of a *theoretically* complete science of physics would be one that affords "a complete, consistent, and unified theory of physical interaction that would describe all possible observations."[3] But to check that the state of physics on hand actually meets this condition, we would need to know exactly what physical interactions are indeed possible. And to warrant us in using the state of physics on hand as a basis for answering this question, we would already have to be assured that its view of the possibilities is correct—and thus already have preestablished its completeness. The idea of a consolidated erotetic completeness shipwrecks on the infeasibility of finding a meaningful way to monitor its attainment.

We can reliably estimate the amount of gold or oil yet to be discovered, because we know a priori the Earth's extent and can thus establish a proportion between what we know and what we do not. But we cannot comparably estimate the amount of knowledge yet to be discovered, because we do not have and cannot have a way of relating what we know to what we do not. The very idea of cognitive limits thus has a paradoxical air. It suggests that we claim knowledge about something outside knowledge. But (to hark back to Hegel) with respect to the realm of knowledge, we are not in a position to draw a line between what lies inside and what lies outside—seeing that, ex hypothesi we have no cognitive access to the latter. One cannot make a survey of the relative extent of knowledge or ignorance about nature except by basing it on some picture of nature that is already in hand—that is, unless one is prepared to take at face value the deliverances of existing science. This process of judging the adequacy of our science on its own telling is the best we can do, but it remains an essentially circular and consequently inconclusive way of proceeding. The long and short of it is that there is no cognitively adequate basis for maintaining the completeness of science in a rationally satisfactory way.

To monitor the theoretical completeness of science, we accordingly need some theory-external control on the adequacy of our theorizing, some theory-external reality-principle to serve as a standard of adequacy. We are thus driven to abandon the road of pure theory and proceed along that of the applicative goals of the enterprise. This gives special importance and urgency to the practical sector.

Pragmatic Completeness

The arbitrament of praxis—not theoretical merit but practical capability—affords the best standard of adequacy for our scientific proceedings that is available. But could we ever be in a position to claim that science has been completed on the basis of the success of its practical applications? On this basis, the perfection of science would have to manifest itself in the perfecting of control—in achieving a perfected technology. But just how are we to proceed here? Could our natural science achieve manifest perfection on the side of control over nature? Could it ever underwrite a recognizably perfected technology?

The issue of "control over nature" involves much more complexity than may appear on first view. For just how is this conception to be understood? Clearly, in terms of bending the course of events to our will, of attaining our ends within nature. But this involvement of "our ends" brings to light the prominence of our own contribution. For example, if we are inordinately modest in our demands (or very unimaginative), we may even achieve "complete control over nature" in the sense of being in a position to do *whatever we want* to do, but yet attain this happy condition in a way that betokens very little real capability.

One might, to be sure, involve the idea of omnipotence and construe a "perfected" technology as one that would enable us to do literally *anything*. But this approach would at once run into the old difficulties already familiar to the medieval scholastics. They were faced with the challenge: "If God is omnipotent, can he annihilate himself (contra his nature as a *necessary* being), or can he do evil deeds (contra his nature as a *perfect* being), or can he make triangles have four angles (contrary to *their* definitive nature)?" Sensibly enough, the scholastics inclined to solve these difficulties by maintaining that an omnipotent God need not be in a position to do literally anything but rather simply anything that it *is possible* for him to do. Similarly, we cannot explicate the idea of technological omnipotence in terms of a capacity to produce any arbitrary result, wholly without qualification. We cannot ask for the production of a *perpetuum mobile*, for spaceships with "hyperdrive" enabling them to attain transluminar velocities, for devices that predict essentially stochastic processes such as the disintegrations of transuranic atoms, or for piston devices that enable us to set *independently* the values for the pressure, temperature, and volume of a body of gas. We cannot, in sum, ask of a "perfected" technology that it should enable us to do anything that we might take into our heads to do, no matter how "unrealistic" this might be.

All that we can reasonably ask is that perfected technology should enable us to do anything *that it is possible for us to do*—and not just what we might *think* we can do, but what we really and truly can do. A perfected technology would be one that enabled us to do anything that *can possibly* be done by creatures circumstanced as we are. But how can we deal with the pivotal conception of "can" that is at issue here? Clearly, only science—real, true, correct, *perfected* science— could tell us what indeed is realistically possible and what circumstances are indeed inescapable. Whenever our "knowledge" falls short of this, we may well "ask the impossible" by way of accomplishment (for example, spaceships in "hyperdrive"), and thus complain of incapacity to achieve control in ways that put unfair burdens on this conception.

Power is a matter of the "effecting of things possible"—of achieving control—and it is clearly cognitive state-of-the-art in science that, in teaching us about the limits of the possible, is itself the agent that must shape our conception of this issue. *Every* law of nature serves to set the boundary between what is genuinely possible and what is not, between what can be done and what cannot, between which questions we can properly ask and which we cannot. We cannot satisfactorily monitor the adequacy and completeness of our science by its ability to effect "all things possible," because science alone can inform us about what is possible. As science grows and develops, it poses new issues of power and control, reformulating and reshaping those demands whose realization represent that key desideratum of "control over nature." For science itself brings new possibilities to light. (At a suitable stage, the idea of "splitting the atom" will no longer seem a contradiction in terms.) To see if a given state of technology meets the condition of perfection, we must *already* have a body of perfected science in hand to tell us what is indeed possible. To validate the claim that our technology is perfected, we need to *preestablish* the completeness of our science. The idea works in such a way that claims to perfected control can rest only on perfected science.

In attempting to travel the practicalist route to cognitive completeness, we are again trapped in a circle, for short of having supposedly perfected science in hand, we could not say what a perfected technology would be like, and thus we could not possibly monitor the perfection of science in terms of the technology that it underwrites.

Moreover, even if (per impossible) a "pragmatic equilibrium" between what we can and what we wish to do in science were to be realized, we could not be warrantedly confident that this condition will remain unchanged. The possibility that just around the corner things will become unstuck can never be eliminated. Even if we "achieve control" to all intents and purposes, we cannot be sure of not losing our grip upon it—not because of a loss of power but because of cognitive changes that produce a broadening of the imagination and a widened apprehension as to what "having control" involves.

Accordingly, the project of achieving practical mastery can never be perfected in a satisfactory way. The point is that control hinges on what we want, and what we want is conditioned by what we think possible, and *this* is something that hinges crucially on theory—on our beliefs about how things work in this world. And so control is something deeply theory infected. We can never safely move from apparent to real adequacy in this regard. We cannot adequately assure that seeming perfection is more than just that. We thus have no alternative but to *presume* that our knowledge (that is, our purported knowledge) is inadequate at this and indeed at any other particular stage of the game of cognitive completeness.

One important point about control must, however, be noted with care. Our preceding negative strictures all relate to attainment of perfect control—of being in a position to do everything possible. No such problems affect the issue of amelioration—of doing some things better and *improving* our control over what it was. It makes perfectly good sense to use its technological applications as standards of scientific advancement. (Indeed, we have no real alternative to using pragmatic standards at this level, because reliance on theory alone is, in the end, going to be circular.) While control does not help us with perfection, it is crucial for monitoring *progress*. Standards of assessment and evaluation are such that we can implement the idea of improvements (progress), but not that of completion (realized perfection). We can determine when we have managed to *enlarge* our technological mastery, but we cannot meaningfully say what it would be to *perfect* it.

Predictive Completeness

The difficulties encountered in using physical control as a standard of "perfection" in science all also hold with respect to *prediction*, which, after all, is simply a mode of *cognitive* control.

Suppose someone asks: "Are you really still going to persist in plaints regarding the incompleteness of scientific knowledge when science can predict *everything?*" The reply is simply that science will *never* be able to predict literally everything: the very idea of predicting *everything* is simply unworkable. For then, whenever we predict something, we would have to predict also the effects of making those predictions, and then the ramification of *those* predictions, and so on ad infinitum. The very most that can be asked is that science put us into a position to predict, not *everything*, but rather *anything* that we might choose to be interested in and to inquire about. And here it must be recognized that our imaginative perception of the possibilities might be much too narrow. We can only make predictions about matters that lie, at least broadly speaking, within our cognitive horizons. Newton could not have predicted findings in quantum theory any more than he could have predicted the outcome of American presidential elections. One can only make predictions about what one is cognizant of, takes note of, or deems worthy of consideration. In this regard, one can be myopic either by not noting or by losing sight of significant sectors of natural phenomena.

To be sure, science itself sets the limits to predictability—insisting that some phenomena (the stochastic processes encountered in quantum physics, for example) are inherently unpredictable. And this is always to some degree problematic. The most that science can reasonably be asked to do is to predict what it sees as in principle predictable—to answer every predictive question that it countenances as proper. And here we must once more recognize that any given state of science might have gotten matters quite wrong.

With regard to predictions, we are thus in the same position that occurs with regard to actually interventionist (rather than "merely cognitive") control. Here, too, we can unproblematically apply the idea of improvement—of progress. But it makes no sense to contemplate the *achievement* of perfection. For its realization is something we could never establish by any practicable means.

Temporal Finality

Scientists from time to time indulge in eschatological musings and tell us that the scientific venture is approaching its end.[4] And it is, of course, entirely conceivable that natural science will come to a stop, and will do so not in consequence of a cessation of intelligent life but in C. S. Peirce's more interesting sense of completion of the project: eventually reaching a condition after which even indefinitely ongoing inquiry will not—and indeed in the very nature of things cannot—produce any significant change, because inquiry has come to "the end of the road." The situation would be analogous to that envisaged in the apocryphal story in vogue during the middle 1800s regarding the commissioner of the United States Patents who resigned his post because there was nothing left to invent.[5]

Such a position is in theory possible. But here, too, we can never determine that it is actual.

There is no practicable way in which the claim that science has achieved temporal finality can be validated. The question, "Is the current state of science, S, final?" is one for which we can never legitimate an affirmative answer. For the prospect of future changes of S can never be precluded. One cannot plausibly move beyond, "We have (in S) no good reason to think that S will ever change" to obtain, "We have (in S) good reason to think that S will never change." To take this posture towards S is to *presuppose its completeness.*[6] It is not simply to take the natural and relatively unproblematic stance that that for which S vouches is to be taken as true, but to go beyond this to insist that whatever is true finds a rationalization within S. This argument accordingly embeds *finality* in *completeness,* and in doing so jumps from the frying pan into the fire. For it shifts from what is difficult to what is even more so. To hold that if something is so at all, then S affords a good reason for it is to take so blatantly ambitious (even megalomaniacal) a view of S that the issue of finality seems almost a harmless appendage.

Moreover, just as the appearance of erotetic and pragmatic equilibrium can be a product of narrowness and weakness, so can temporal finality. We may think that science is unchangeable simply because we have been unable to change it. But that's just not good enough. Were science ever to come to a seeming stop, we could never be sure that it had done so not because it is at "the end of the road" but because we are at the end of our tether. We can never ascertain that science has attained the ω-condition of final completion, since from our point of view the possibility of further change lying "just around the corner" can never be ruled out finally and decisively. No matter how final a position we *appear* to have reached, the prospects of its coming unstuck cannot be precluded. As we have seen, future science is inscrutable. We can never claim with assurance that the position we espouse is immune to change under the impact of further data—that the oscillations are dying out and we are approaching a final limit. In its very nature, science "in the limit" relates to what happens in the long run, and this is something about which we *in principle* cannot gather information: any information we can actually gather inevitably pertains to the short run and not the long run. We can never achieve adequate assurance that *apparent* definitiveness is *real*. We can never consolidate the claim that science has settled into a frozen, changeless pattern. The situation in natural science is such that our knowledge of nature must ever be presumed to be incomplete.

The idea of achieving a state of recognizably completed science is totally unrealistic. Even as widely variant modes of behavior by three dimensional objects could produce exactly the same two-dimensional shadow-projections, so too could very different law-systems, in principle, engender exactly the same phenomena. We cannot make any definitive inferences from phenomena to the nature of the real. The prospect of perfected science is bound to elude us. The upshot is that science must always be presumed to be incomplete.

One of the clearest lessons of the history of science is that where scientific knowledge is concerned, further discovery does not just *supplement* but generally *emends* our prior information. Accordingly, we have little alternative but to take the humbling view that the incompleteness of our purported knowledge about the world entails its potential incorrectness as well. It is now a matter not simply of *gaps* in the structure of our knowledge or errors of omission. There is no realistic alternative but to suppose that we face a situation of real *flaws* as well, of errors of commission. This aspect of the matter endows incompleteness with an import graver than might appear on first view.[7]

The Dispensability of Perfection

The cognitive situation of natural science invites description in theological terms. The ambiguity of the human condition is only too manifest here. We cannot expect ever to reach a position of definitive finality in this imperfect dispensation: we do have "knowledge" of sorts, but it is manifestly imperfect. Expelled from the Garden of Eden, we are deprived of access to "the God's-eye point of view." Definitive and comprehensive adequacy is denied us: we have no basis for claiming to know "the truth, the whole truth, and nothing but the truth" in scientific matters. We yearn for absolutes, but have to settle for plausibilities; we desire what is definitively correct, but have to settle for conjectures and estimates.

In this imperfect epistemic dispensation, we have to reckon with the realities of the human condition. Age disagrees with age; different states of the art involve naturally discordant conceptions and incommensurate positions. The moral of the story of the Tower of Babel applies.

The absolutes for which we yearn represent an ideal that lies beyond the range of practicable realization. We simply have to do the best we can with the means at our disposal. To aspire to absolutes—for definitive comprehensiveness—is simply unrealistic.

It is sometimes maintained that such a fallibilist and imperfectionist view of science is unacceptable. To think of science as *inevitably* incomplete and to think of "the definitive answers" in scientific matters as *perpetually* unattainable is, we are told, to write science off as a meaningful project.

But in science as in the moral life, we can operate perfectly well in the realization that perfection is unattainable. No doubt here and there some scientists nurse the secret hope of attaining some fixed and final definitive result that will stand, untouchable and changeless, through all subsequent ages. But unrealistic aspirations are surely by no means essential to the scientific enterprise as such. In science, as in other domains of human endeavor, it is a matter of doing the best we can with the tools at hand.

For the fact that *perfection* is unattainable does nothing to countervail the no less real fact that *improvement* is realizable—that progress is possible. The undeniable prospect of realizable progress—of overcoming genuine defect and deficiencies that we find in the work of our predecessors—affords ample impetus to scientific innovation. Scientific progress is not generated *a fronte* by the pull of an unattainable ideal; it is stimulated *a tergo* by the push of dissatisfaction with the deficiencies of achieved positions. The labors of science are not pulled forward by the mirage of (unattainable) perfection. We are pushed onward by the (perfectly realizable) wish to do better than our predecessors in the enterprise.

We can understand "progress" in two senses. On the one hand, there is O-progress, defined in terms of increasing distance from the starting point (the "origin"). On the other hand, there is D-progress, defined in terms of decreasing distance from the goal (the "destination.") Consider the picture:

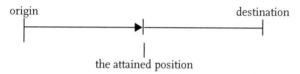

Ordinarily, the two modes of progress are entirely equivalent: we increase the distance traveled from O by exactly the same amount as we decrease the distance remained to D. But if there is no attainable destination—if we are engaged on a journey that, for all we know, is literally endless and has no determinable destination, or only one that is "infinitely distant"—then we just cannot manage to decrease our distance from it.

Given that in natural science we embarked on a journey that is literally endless, it is only O-progress that can be achieved, and not D-progress. We can gauge our progress only in terms of how far we have come, and not in terms of how far we have to go. On a journey that is in principle endless, we simply cannot say that we are nearing the goal.

The upshot is straightforward. The idea of *improving* our science can be implemented without difficulty, since we can clearly improve our performance as regards its goals of prediction, control, and the rest. But the idea of *perfecting* our science cannot be implemented.

The idea of "perfected science" is that *focus imaginarius* whose pursuit canalizes and structures our theorizing. It represents the ultimate telos of inquiry, the idealized destination of a journey in which we are still and indeed are ever engaged, a grail of sorts that we can pursue but not possess. The ideal of perfection thus serves a fundamentally regulative role to mark the fact that actuality falls short of our cognitive aspirations. It marks a contrast that regulates how we make and must view our claims, playing a rule akin to that of the functionary who reminded the Roman emperor of his mortality in reminding us that our pretensions are always vulnerable. Contemplation of this idea reminds us that the human condition is suspended between the reality of imperfect achievement and the ideal of an unattainable perfection. In abandoning this conception—in rejecting the idea of an "ideal science" that alone can properly be claimed to afford a definitive grasp of reality—we would abandon an idea that crucially regulates our view regarding the nature and status of the knowledge to which we lay claim. We would then no longer be constrained to characterize our view of things as *merely* ostensible and purported. We would be tempted to regard our picture of nature as real, authentic, and final in a manner that we, at bottom, realize it does not deserve.

What is being maintained here is not that "completed and perfected science" is a senseless conception as such, but rather that the idea of *attaining* it is senseless. It represents a theoretically realizable state whose actual realization we can never achieve. What is unrealizable is not perfection as such but the *epistemic condition* of recognizing its attainment. (Even if we arrive, we can never tell that we're there!)

But does this situation not destroy "the pursuit of perfection" as a meaningful endeavor? Here it is useful to heed the distinction between a *goal* and an *ideal*. A goal is something that we hope and expect to achieve. An ideal is merely a wistful inkling, a "wouldn't it be nice if"—something that figures in the mode of aspiration rather than expectation. A goal motivates us in striving for its attainment; an ideal stimulates and encourages. And ideal does not provide us with a destination that we have any expectation of reaching; it is something for whose actual attainment we do not even hope. It is in *this* sense that "perfected science" is an ideal.[8]

Here, as elsewhere, we must reckon appropriately with the standard gap between aspiration and attainment. In the practical sphere—in craftsmanship, for example, or the cultivation of our health—we may *strive* for perfection, but cannot ever claim to *attain* it. And the situation in inquiry is exactly parallel with what we encounter in such other domains—ethics specifically included. The value of an ideal, even of one that is not realizable, lies not in the benefit of its attainment (obviously and ex hypothesi!) but in the benefits that accrue from its pursuit. The view that it is rational to pursue an aim only if we are in a position to achieve its attainment or approximation is mistaken; it can be perfectly valid (and entirely rational) if the indirect benefits of its pursuit and adoption are sufficient—if in striving after it, we realize relevant advantages to a substantial degree. An unattainable ideal can be enormously productive. And so, the legitimation of the idea of "perfected science" lies in its facilitation of the ongoing evolution of inquiry. In this domain, we arrive at the perhaps odd-seeming posture of an invocation of practical utility for the validation of an ideal.

4

Realism/Idealism

Realism and Its Limits

The position of metaphysical realism stands essentially as follows:

> Reality is mind independent. We live in a world not of our own making, a world whose constituents and their modes of operation are independent of our thought. Thought and its machinations have no bearing on the constituents and laws of nature, which are what they are independently of the existence of thinking beings.

This sort of realism is not without its difficulties. One of its limitations lies in the crucial distinction between *that* and *what*. For it is one thing to claim abstractly and indefinitely *that* there is a domain of mind-independent reality, and something quite different to make claims regarding *what* it is like.

In stating any descriptively concrete claims about the world's realities, we have no alternative but to employ man-contrived languages and the thought-control ideas and concepts that they embody.

And leaving behind the self-subsistent realm of reality itself, we now have to enter into the sphere of human beliefs about it. And here the inherent nature of thought becomes unavoidable. The instruction, "Tell me what is the case about something, really and truly, quite apart from what you think and believe to be so" issues an inherently unmeetable demand. Our only cognitive access to what there is proceeds through the doorway of what we think to be so. Metaphysical realism, seen abstractly, is all very well in its way, but when it comes to the question of just what it is that we are being realistic about, it would seem that we must be prepared to let idealism have its say.

Idealism and Its Modes

Idealism, broadly speaking, is the doctrine that reality is somehow mind-correlative or mind-coordinated. Bertrand Russell once said that "idealists tell us that what appears as matter is really something mental."[1] But that is slightly stretching things. Idealism certainly need not go so far as to maintain a causal theory to the effect that mind somehow *makes* or *constitutes* matter—let alone that reality *is* mental. This oversimple view of idealism ignores such versions of the theory as, for example, the explanatory idealism, which merely holds that an adequate *explanation* of the real is unachievable in the absence of some recourse to the operations of the mind.

A more modest and sensible idealism will merely have it that reality as we understand it reflects the workings of the mind. And it will take this to mean that the comprehending mind itself makes a formative contribution not merely to our understanding of the nature of the real, but even to the descriptive character that we attribute to it. Such an idealism regards the natural world as a system that makes possible and perhaps even probable the developmental pathway of intelligent beings that can grasp the world's modus operandi. Thought thus gains its key position in reality not by virtue of the primacy of creating it, but rather by virtue of the emergent saliency of its role in nature. And in this light it is unjust to charge idealism with an antipathy to reality, with ontophobia, as Ortega y Gasset called it. For it is not the *existence* but the *nature* of reality upon which idealism sets its sights.

Conceptual Idealism

The specifically *conceptual*—rather than substantive—idealism that is now at issue maintains that any adequate descriptive characterization of physical ("material") reality must at some point involve an implicit reference to mental operations—that some commerce with mental characteristics and operations always occurs in any viable explanatory exposition of "the real world."[2] The central thesis of this position is that the mind is responsible for nature as we understand it, not, to be sure, by making nature itself, but rather through its formative role in providing the mode- and manner-determining categories in whose terms its conception is cast. With such an approach, the constitutive role of the mind in nature is to be thought of neither in ontological nor causal terms but hermeneutically by way of concept explication. It is not that mind produces nature, but rather that the manner of its conceptualization of nature involves the analogy of mind; in sum, that we conceive of the real in mind-correlative terms of reference.

Such a conceptual idealism's central thesis is that the salient characterizing properties ascribed to physical things in our standard conceptual scheme are at bottom all *relational* properties, with some facet of "the mind"—or of minds in general—serving as one term of this relation. Specifically, it holds that the concept or scheme that we standardly use to construe our experience ascribes properties and characteristics to "material" objects that involve some reference to mental operations within the very meaning of the terms at issue. Let us consider how this is so.

Conceptual idealism is predicated upon the important distinction between conceptual mind-involvingness and explicit mind-invokingness, illustrated in the contrast between a book and a dream. To characterize an object of consideration as a *dream* or a *worry* is explicitly mind-invoking. For dreams and worries exist only where there is dreaming and worrying, which, by their very nature, typify the sorts of things at issue in the thought processes of mind-endowed creatures: where there are dreams or worries, these must be mind-equipped beings to do the dreaming and worrying. A book, by contrast, seems at first sight entirely nonmental: books, after all, unlike dreams or worries, are physical objects. If mind-endowed beings were to vanish from the world, dreams and worries would vanish with them—but seemingly not books! Even if there were no mind-endowed beings, there could certainly be naturally evolved book-like objects, objects *physically indistinguishable from books as we know them.* Nevertheless, there could not be books in a world where minds have no existence. For a book is, by definition, an artifact purposively conceived, equipped with pages on which "reading material" is printed. Such purposive artifacts all invoke goal-directed processes of a type that can exist only where there are minds. To be a book is to have *writing* within, not just *marks.* And writing is inherently the sort of thing produced and employed by mind-endowed beings. In sum, to explain adequately what a book is we must thus make reference to writing and ultimately to minds.

The salient point here is not that the book is mentalesque as a physical object, but rather that to explicate what is involved in characterizing that object as "a book"—to characterize what it is to be a book—we must eventually refer to minds and their capabilities, seeing that, given our understanding of what is at issue, a book is by its very nature something for people to read. A world without minds can contain objects physically indistinguishable from our books and nails, but *books* and *nails* they would not and could not be, since only artifacts created for a certain sort of intelligence-invoking purpose can correctly be characterized as such. The status of those objects as books or nails is mind-conducted. And so, while books—unlike dreams—are not mental items, their conceptualization/characterization must nevertheless be cast in mind-involving terms of reference. To be a book is to be a thing that functions in an ineliminably mind-related way. Books as such can only exist in mind-affording contexts.

This conception of the tacitly mind-involving (as contrasted with the explicitly mind-invoking) will be central in these deliberations. For it maintains that even the physical properties of things are themselves mind-involving in the analytic sense that their explicative conceptual unpacking calls for a reference to minds and their capabilities.

The pivotal thesis of conceptual idealism is accordingly that we standardly think of reality in implicitly mentalesque terms. And this contention rests on two basic theses:

1. That *our* world, the world as we know it, is—inevitably—the world *as we conceive it to be*, and

2. That the pivotal concepts (thought-instrumentalities) that we standardly use in characterizing and describing this world contain in their make-up, somewhere along the line, a reference to the operations of mind.

Observing that our "standard conception" of the world we live in is that of a multitude of particulars endowed with empirical properties and positioned in space and time and interacting causally, conceptual idealism goes on to maintain that all of the salient conceptions operative here—particularity, spatiotemporality, causality, and the possession of empirical (experimentally accessible) properties—are mind-involving in exactly the sense explicated above.

The most common objection to idealism in general centers on the issue of the mind-independence of the real. "Surely," so runs the objection, "things in nature would remain substantially unchanged if there were no minds. Had intelligent creatures never evolved on the earth, its mountains and valleys would nevertheless be much as they are, and the sun and moon remain substantially unaffected." This contention is perfectly plausible in one aspect, namely the *causal* one—which is just why causal idealism has its problems. The crucial mind-independence of the real has to be granted in the causal mode. But not in the conceptual mode. For the objection's exponent has to face the question of specifying just exactly what it is that would remain the same. "Surely roses would smell just as sweet in a mind-denuded world!" Well, yes and no. The absence of minds would not change roses, but rose fragrance and sweetness—and even the size and shape of roses—are all features whose character hinges on such mind-invoking operations as smelling, scanning, comparing, measuring, and the like. For something really to be a rose it must, unavoidably, have various capacities to evoke mental responses—it must admit of identification, specification, classification, and property attribution, and these, by their very nature, are all mental operations. Striking people as being rose-like is critical to qualifying as a rose; if seemingly rose bushes performed strangely—say by sprouting geranium like flowers—they would no longer be so: rose bushes just don't do that sort of thing. A rose that is not conceived of in mind-referential terms is—not a rose at all.

Within the present confines, there is not room enough to tell the whole story, so one key part of it will have to do. We still begin at the beginning—particularity. So a base sketch will have to do. Thus, particularity is a matter of identification, spatiotemporally a matter of orientation, causality a matter of explanation, and property possession a matter of description. And all of these are mind-involving processes. All of these are implicitly mind-involving activities that envision the world's operations in terms of characteristically mental processes. The world *as we conceive it* is a mental artifact that is constructed (in part) in mind-referential terms—the nature of the world as we conceive of it reflects the workings of the mind.

Of course, in speaking of mind-involvement or mind-invocation, no reference to any particular mind is at issue. The operative mental aspect here is not private or personal: it is not a question of *whose* mind—of this or that mind rather than another. The dependence at issue is wholly generic and systematic in nature.

In this way, then, conceptual idealism's position is that the realm of matter as we conceive of it is mind-involving. For it holds that our standard conception of particular concrete objects—things located in space and time and interacting with one another—is shot through with mind-invoking involvements. But this entire argument that the mind is basic for matter as holding in the conceptual order is based on the idea that a mind-invoking conception is one whose ultimate analysis demands a reference to minds or their capabilities.

And so, *conceptual* idealism sees the mind not as *causal source* of the materials of nature but as indispensably furnishing some of the *interpretative mechanisms* in whose terms we understand them. It is predicated on the view that reality as we standardly conceive it—in terms of material objects identifiable through discernible dispositional properties, causally interacting with one another in the setting of space and time—is thereby unavoidably enmeshed with the operations of the mind. It maintains that the mind understands nature in a manner that, in some ways, reflects its own operations in fundamental respects—that we come to cognitive grips with nature on our own terms, that is, in terms of concepts whose makeup involves some reference to minds and their operations. The position rests squarely on the classical idealistic doctrine that the mind contributes essentially to the constitution—as well as the constituting—of our knowledge of reality.

It is sometimes said that idealism is predicated on a confusion of objects with our knowledge of them and conflates the real with our thought about it. But this charge misses the point when a conceptual idealism is at issue. Conceptual idealism's thesis is not the trivial one that what the mind makes is merely the *idea* of nature; it is not open to Santayana's complaint against Schopenhauer that "he proclaimed that the world was his idea, but meant only (what is undeniable) that his *idea* of the world was his idea." To say that we can only obtain a view of reality via its representations by the mind is true but trivial—we can only obtain a mind-provided view of anything whatsoever. But to say that our view of reality (as standardly articulated) is one that represents reality by means of concepts and categories that are mind-referring in their nature is certainly not trivial. And it is this position that is at stake in the conceptual idealism that is now at issue. What is at issue is that mind-patterned conceptions are built into our very idea of nature—that what this idea involves is itself limited to mental operation.

Problems of Mind and Matter

The following sort of objection against a conceptual idealism may well be offered: "How can one sensibly maintain the mind dependency of matter as ordinarily conceived, when all the world recognizes that the operations of the mind are based on the machinations of matter?" However, this objection simply gets things wrong. There just is no question of any real conflict once the proper distinctions have been drawn, because—as indicated above—altogether different sorts of dependencies or requirements are at issue in the two theses:

1. That mind is *causally* dependent upon (that is, causally requires) matter, in that mental process demands *causally* or productively the physical workings of matter.

2. That matter (conceived of in the standard manner of material substance subject to physical law) is *explicatively* dependent upon (that is, *conceptually* requires) the mind, in that the conception of material processes involves *hermeneutically* or semantically the mentalistic working of the mind.

We return here to the crucial distinction between the conceptual order, with its essentially hermeneutic or *explicative* perspective upon the intellectual exposition of meanings, and the *causal* order, with its *explanatory* perspective upon the productive efficacy of physical processes. In the hermeneutic framework of consideration, our concern is not with any facets of the causal explanation of intellectual processes, but instead it is with understanding these processes from within, on their own terms—in the conceptual order. The issue is not one of *causal explanation* at all, but one of *understanding* achieved through an analysis of the internal meaning-content of concepts and of the semantic *information* conveyed by statements in which they are operative.

Because of the fundamental difference between these two perspectives of consideration, any conflict in the dependency relations to which they give rise is altogether harmless from the standpoint of actual inconsistency. The circle breaks because *different* modes of dependency are involved: we move from mind to matter in the conceptual order of understanding (of *rationes cognoscendi* or rather *concipiendi*) and from matter to mind in the ontologically dependent order of causation (*rationes essendi*). Once all the due distinctions are duly heeded, any semblance of vicious circularity disappears. No doubt, this calls for a certain amount of care and subtlety—but then so do many issues of intellectual life and why should things be easier in philosophy than elsewhere?

To some extent then, the conceptual idealist's thesis is that one specific direction of dependence (that of the physical upon that of the mental) is built into the view of reality at issue in our standard conceptual scheme. But this must not be seen as conflicting with the debatable (but by no means thereby negligible) prospect that the scientific explanation of causal relationships might envision a reversal in the direction of dependence. Where different perspectives are involved, seemingly conflicting theses are perfectly compatible. (I can say without conflict that my car is economical in point of gas mileage and uneconomical in point of maintenance costs.)

Yet even if no vicious circle arises, do we not arrive at an equally vicious infinite regress that altogether precludes understanding. For is understandability not precluded from the outset if an adequate overall understanding of the mind requires reference to its causal origins in matter, and an adequate overall understanding of matter requires reference to its functional presuppositions of a mind-invoking sort? The answer is negative. A problematic regress would arise here only if one adopted an essentially linear model of understanding. But this is quite inappropriate in the case of *coordinated* concepts such as the present instance of mind/matter or the simpler case of cause/effect. To say that we cannot fully understand the cause until we understand its effect, and that we cannot fully understand the effect until we understand the cause, is not to show that there is a vitiating regress with the result that we cannot understand either one. All it shows is that two such coordinated and interrelated concepts cannot be set out through a *sequential* explanation but must be grasped *together* in their systematic unity.

A somewhat crude analogy may be helpful at this point. Take a knife and its blade. If an object is to count as a knife, then the shiny thing attached to the handle must be a blade, but this thing cannot count as a blade unless the whole it comprises together with that handle is a knife. The two items stand in conceptually symbiotic apposition: X cannot be properly characterized as X unless it is duly related to Y, and Y cannot be properly characterized as such unless it is duly related to X. We cannot pick up either end of the stick without avoiding the other. We must grasp the whole in one fell swoop. Just such a cognitive *coordination* of mentalistic and materialistic concepts holds with respect to our present analysis of their mutual interdependencies. But interdependency does not annihilate difference, and by maintaining due distinctions, any collapse into vicious circularity or vitiating regress can be avoided.

Conceptual idealism is thus even compatible with a causal materialism that maintains matter to be basic to the mind in the causal order. On the causal issues of the origins of the mind, conceptualistic idealism is silent and so compatible with various theories—materialism itself not excluded. Conceptual idealism just is not an *explanatory* theory regarding the causal mechanisms of the mind's processes or mode of origination; it is an *analytical* theory regarding the nature of the conceptual mechanisms of the categories of understanding. It can thus coexist with *any* theory of the mind that is articulated along strictly *causal* lines—be it a Cartesian-style dualism of reciprocal influence or even a unidirectional epiphenomenalism.

The conceptual idealist accordingly has no vested interest in denying a "scientistic" view that the mind and its functioning may ultimately prove to be somehow causally emergent from the processes of matter. The position does not need to be argued through an attack upon causal materialism: it is quite compatible with the idea that mental functioning has its material basis and causal origins in the realm of physical processes. The doctrine's point is simply that our standard conception of the world—its material sector specifically included—is forthcoming in terms of reference that are at bottom mind-involving. It is the analytical issue of *how we actually think* of the world, not the operational issue of the mechanics of its causal goings-on that constitutes the focus of concern. Of course, any currently viable form of idealism has to make its peace with science and come to terms with the world as the science of the day depicts it. And in particular it must accept the theory of evolution—cosmic and biological alike—and come to terms with a universe that initially dispensed even with solid state physics (to say nothing of chemistry, let alone biology). In such a universe, the emergence of mind comes late in the day; mind is but a "Johnny-come-lately." And this too is something that a conceptual idealism can manage to take in stride.

In sum, then, a cogent case can be made for holding that the familiar objections to idealism—traditional and recent alike—can be defused when one makes a shift from an *ontological* to the *conceptualistic* version of the doctrine, which, to all appearances, seems to offer the best prospect of acceptability.

5

Intelligent Design

Being Intelligently Designed

Two key ideas guide the present discussion: (1) that there is a substantial difference between being designed *intelligently* and being designed *by intelligence*, and (2) that evolution, broadly understood, is in principle a developmental process through which the former feature—being designed intelligently—can actually be realized. The conjoining of these items means that, rather than there being a conflict or opposition between evolution and intelligent design, evolution itself can be conceived of as an instrumentality of intelligent design.

To be intelligently designed is to be constituted in the way an intelligent being *would* arrange it. To this end, it need certainly not be claimed that an intelligent being *did* do so. Being intelligently designed no more requires an intelligent designer than being designed awkwardly requires an awkward one.

At bottom, intelligent design is a matter of efficiency and effectiveness in goal realization. But what can be said when the entire universe is at issue? How are we to conceive of this matter of aims and goals then? The crux of the matter is not afforded by the question, "Does the universe have a goal?" but rather by the subtler, purely conditional and *strictly hypothetical* question: "If we are to think of the universe as having a goal, then what could it reasonably be?" The issue here is one of a figuratively *virtual* rather than an actually *literal* goal.

So to begin, we must ask whether or not it is reasonable to expect an intelligent agent or agency to produce a certain result. Clearly, this issue will depend on the aims and purposes this agent or agency could reasonably be expected to have. And this leads to the question: "What is it that one could reasonably expect regarding the productive aims and purposes of an intelligent agent or agency?"

Now what would obviously have pride of place in the evaluative pantheon of such an intelligence is intelligence itself. Surely nothing has higher value for an intelligent being than intelligence itself, and there is little that would be worse for a being than "losing its reason." Intelligence and rationality are the paramount values for any rational creature: a rational being would rather lose its right arm than lose its reason.

But of course a rational being will thereby only value something it regards as *having* value; it would not value something that it did not deem valuable. Thus, it will only value rationality in itself if it deems rationality itself to be something of value. And so in valuing their rationality, truly rational creatures are bound to value rationality in general—whenever it may be found. The result of this will be a reciprocal recognizance among rational beings—as such, they are bound to see themselves as the justly proud bearers of a resource of special value.

Accordingly, the only response to the question of a goal for world development that has a scintilla of plausibility would have to take the essentially Hegelian line of locating the crux of intelligent design in the very factor of intelligence itself. Implementing this idea calls for locating the "virtual" goal of the universe within its providing for the development of intelligent beings able to achieve some understanding of its own ways and operations. One would accordingly inquire whether the world's nature and modus operandi are so constituted as to lead with efficiency and effectiveness to the emergence of intelligent beings. Put in technical jargon the question becomes: is the universe noophelic—that is, intelligence friendly—in favoring the interests of intelligence in the course of its development?

A positive response here has deep roots in classical antiquity—originally in Plato and Aristotle and subsequently in the Aristotelian neo-Platonism of Plotinus and Proclus. And it emerges when two ancient ideas are put into juxtaposition—first, it is love that makes the world go round, and the second is that such love is a matter of understanding, so its crux lies in an *amor intellecualis* of sorts.[1] On this perspective, self-understanding, the appreciation through intelligence of intelligence, would be seen as definitive aim and telos of nature's ongoing self-development. Such a position is, in effect, that of an updated neo-Platonism. And it represents a tendency of thought that still has potential relevancy.

Nature's Noophelia

From this perspective, intelligent design calls for the prospering of intelligence in the world's scheme of things. But just what would this involve?

Of course the emergence of living organisms is a crucial factor here. And an organically *viable* environment—to say nothing of a cognitively *knowable* one—must incorporate orderly experiential structures. There must be regular patterns of occurrence in nature that even simple, single-celled creatures can embody in their make-up and reflect in their operations. Even the humblest organisms, snails, say, and even algae, must so operate that certain types of stimuli (patterns of recurrently discernible impacts) call forth appropriately corresponding types of responses—that such organisms can detect structural patterns in their natural environment and react to it in a way that proves to their advantage in evolutionary terms. Even its simplest creatures can maintain themselves in existence only by swimming in a sea of regularities of exactly the sort that would be readily detectable by intelligence. And so nature must cooperate with intelligence in a very particular way—it must be stable enough, regular enough, and structured enough for there to be appropriate responses to natural events that can be "learned" by creatures. If such "appropriate responses" are to develop, nature must provide suitable stimuli in a duly structured way. Nature must thus present us with an environment that affords sufficiently stable patterns to make coherent "experience" possible, enabling us to derive appropriate *information* from our structured interactions with the environment. Accordingly, a world in which any form of intelligence evolves will have to be a world whose processes bring grist to the mill of intelligence. To reemphasize: *A world in which intelligent creatures emerge in a natural and efficient way through the operation of evolutionary processes must be a substantially intelligible world.*

But there is another side to it above and beyond intelligible order. For the world must also be varied and diversified—it cannot be so bland and monotone that the stimulation of challenge and response processes required for evolution is not forthcoming. Evolution itself requires that a universe containing intelligent creatures must be intelligence-congenial: it must be just the sort of universe that an intelligent creature would—if it could—endeavor to contrive, a universe that is intelligently designed with a view to the existence and flourishing of intelligent beings.

A world in which intelligence emerges by anything like standard evolutionary processes must be a realm pervaded by regularities and periodicities regarding organism-nature interaction that produces and perpetuates organic species. And so, to possibilize the evolutionary emergence of intelligent beings the universe must afford a manifold of lawful order that makes it a cosmos rather than a chaos.

In sum then, a complex world with organisms that develop by natural selection is not only going to be such that intelligent beings are likely to emerge, but is, in fact, going to be an intelligently designed world. Accordingly, four facts speak most prominently on behalf of a noophelic cosmos:

- The fact that the world's realities proceed and develop under the aegis of natural laws: that it is a manifold of lawful order whose doings exhibit a self-perpetuating stability of processual function.

- The fact of a course of cosmic development that has seen an ever-growing scope for manifolds of lawful order, providing step-by-step the materials for the development of the laws of physics, their theme of chemistry, their biology, their sociology, and so on.

- The fact that intelligent beings have in fact emerged—that nature's modus operandi has possibilized and facilitated the emergence of intelligence.

- The fact of an ever-deepening comprehension and penetration of nature's ways on the part of intelligent beings—their ongoing expansion and deepening of their understanding of the world's events and processes.

And so, the key that unlocks all of these large explanatory issues regarding the nature of the world is the very presence of intelligent beings upon its stage. For if intelligence is to emerge in a world by evolutionary means, it becomes a requisite that that world must be substantially intelligible. It must comport itself in a way that intelligent beings can grasp, and thereby function in a way that is substantially regular, orderly, economical, and rational. In sum, it must be the sort of world that intelligent beings would contrive if they themselves were world contrivers, so that the world must be "as though" it were the product of an intelligent agent or agency; although there is no way to take the iffiness of that "as though" out of it.

In sum, evolutionary noophelia is a position for which there is plausible basis of evidential substantiation. Intelligence too needs its nourishment. In a world without significantly diversified phenomena intelligent creatures would lack opportunities for development. If their lifespan is too short, they cannot learn. If too long, there is too slow a pace of generational turnover for effective development—a sort of cognitive arteriosclerosis. Accordingly, nature's own contribution to the issue of the intelligibility of nature has to be the possession of a relatively simple, uniform, and systematic law structure with regard to its processes—one that deploys so uncomplicated a set of regularities that even a community of inquirers possessed of only rather modest capabilities can be expected to achieve a fairly good grasp of significant parts of it.

On this line of deliberation, nature admits cognitive access not just because it has laws (is a *cosmos*), but because it has *relatively sim-*

ple laws. And these relatively simple laws must be there because if they were not, then nature just could not afford a viable environment for intelligent life. But how might an intelligence-friendly, *noophelic* world come about? At this point evolution comes upon the stage of deliberation.

In order to emerge to prominence through evolution, intelligence must give an "evolutionary edge" to its possessors. The world must encapsulate straightforwardly "learnable" patterns and periodicities of occurrence in its operations—relatively simply laws. A world that is too anarchic or chaotic for reason to get a firm grasp on the modus operandi of things will be a world in which intelligent beings cannot emerge through the operations of evolutionary mechanisms. In a world that is not substantially lawful, they cannot emerge. In a world whose law structure is not in many ways rather simple, they cannot function effectively.

There are many ways in which an organic species can endure across generations—the *multiplicity* of sea turtles, the *speed* of gazelles, the *hardness* of tortoise shells, and the *simplicity* of microorganisms all afford examples. But among these survival strategies, intelligence—the resource of intelligent beings—is an adaptive instrumentality of potent and indeed potentially optimal efficacy and effectiveness. So in a universe that is sufficiently fertile and complex, the emergence of intelligent beings can be seen as something that is "only natural" under the pressure of evolutionary processes.

In sum, for nature to be intelligible there must be a coordinative alignment that requires cooperation on both sides. The analogy of cryptanalysis is suggestive. If *A* is to break *B*'s code, there must be due reciprocal alignment. If *A*'s methods are too crude, too hit-and-miss, he can get nowhere. But even if *A* is quite intelligent and resourceful, his efforts cannot succeed if *B*'s procedures are simply beyond his powers. (The cryptanalysts of the 17th century, clever though they were, could get absolutely nowhere in applying their investigative instrumentalities to a high-level naval code of World War II vintage.) Analogously, if the mind and nature were too far out of alignment—if the mind were "too unintelligent" for the complexities of nature or nature "too complex" for the capacities of the mind—the two just couldn't get into step. It would be like trying to rewrite

Shakespeare in a pidgin English with a five hundred word vocabulary or like trying to monitor the workings of a system containing ten degrees of freedom by using a cognitive mechanism capable of keeping track of only four of them. If something like this were the case, the mind could not accomplish its evolutionary mission. The interests of survival would then have been better served by an alignment process that does not take the cognitive route. And so, if the development of intelligent beings is the aim, then evolution is a pretty effective means for its realization. What we have is a hermeneutic circle in which evolution productively explains the operandi of intelligence, while intelligence functionally explains the operation of evolution.

And so, what evolution does by natural selection is to take some of the magic out of intelligence—to help demystify that presence of intelligence in the cosmos. It is no more surprising that nature provides grist for the mind than that it provides food for the body. But it manages to do this precisely to the extent that it qualifies as an intelligently construed instrumentality for the realization of intelligence.

Nature's Nootropism

Beyond the issue of the evolution *of* intelligence there is also that of intelligence *in* evolution.

The question from which we set out was: is the world so constituted that its natural development leads with effectiveness and efficacy to the emergence of intelligent beings able to achieve some understanding of its modus operandi? And the answer to this question as we have envisioned it lies in the consideration that a world in which intelligent creatures emerge through evolutionary means—as ours actually seems to be—is pretty much bound to be so constituted.

A universe designed *by* an intelligent being would accordingly be a universe designed *for* intelligent beings and thus be user-friendly for intelligent beings. Their very rationality requires rational beings to see themselves as members of a confraternity of a special and particularly worthy kind. But what about rationality in nature?

One would certainly expect on general principles that the nature's processes should proceed in a maximally effective way—on the whole and with everything considered comporting itself intelligently, subject to considerations of what might be characterized as a rational economy of effort. And so, with rationality understood as being a matter of the intelligent management of appropriate proceedings, we would view nature as a fundamentally rational system. However, our expectation of such processual rationality is not based on *personifying* nature but, to the contrary, on *naturalizing* intelligence. For to say that nature comports itself intelligently is not so much to model nature in our image as it is to position ourselves within the manifold of processes that is natural to nature itself. Here there is no projection of our intelligence into nature, but rather of envisioning a (minute) manifestation of nature's intelligence in ourselves. Nature's inclination to promote intelligence and its interests—nootropism in short—is thus to be seen as perfectly *naturalistic*, an aspect of its inherent modus operandi.[2] For in seeing its workings to proceed *as though* intelligent agency were at work, we not so much conceive of nature in our terms of reference as conceive of ourselves as natural products of the fundamentally rational comportment of nature. Our rationality, insofar as we possess it, is simply an inherent part of nature's ratiotropism, so that the result is not an anthropomorphism of nature but rather a naturomorphism of man.

When desirable outcomes of extremely small probability are being produced with undue frequency we can count on it that some sort of cheating is going on.[3] And on this basis it would appear that nature "cheats" by exhibiting a favorable bias towards the interests of intelligence by functioning as to render an intelligence-favorable result more probable than would otherwise be the case. Indeed the noophelia that figures among rationality's most basic commitments is among the most striking features of nature's modus operandi.

A Naturalistic Teleology

It would be a profound error to oppose evolution to intelligent design—to see them as somehow conflicting and incompatible. For natural selection—the survival of forms better able to realize self-replication in the face of challenges and overcome the difficulties posed by the world's vicissitudes—affords an effective means to establishing intelligent resolutions. (It is no accident that whales and sophisticated computer-designed submarines share much the same physical configuration or that the age of iron succeeded that of bronze.) The process of *natural* selection at work in the unfolding of biological evolution is replicated in the *rational* selection we encounter throughout the history of human artifice. On either side, evolution reflects the capacity to overcome obstacles and resolve problems in the direction of greater efficiency and effectiveness. Selective evolutionary pressures—alike in natural (biological) and rational (cultural) selection—are thus instrumentalities that selectively move the developmental course of things toward increasing rationality.

Yet, why should it be that the universe is so constituted as to permit the emergence of intelligence? Three possible answers to the problem of nature's user-friendliness toward intelligence suggest themselves:

- The universe itself is the product of the creative agency of an intelligent being who, as such, will of course favor the interests of intelligence.

- Our universe is simply one item within a vast multiverse of alternatives—and it just so happens (fortuitously, as it were) that the universe that we ourselves inhabit is one that exhibits intelligent design and intelligence-friendliness.

- Any manifold able to constitute a universe that is self-propagating and self- perpetuating over time is bound to develop, in due course, an intelligence-favoring dimension. The same sort of selective developmental pressures that make for the emergence of intelligent beings *in* the universe make for the emergence of an intelligent design *of* the universe.

Note that the first and the last of these prospects are perfectly compatible, though both explanations would be incompatible with the middle alternative whose bizarre character marks its status as that of a decidedly desperate recourse.

To be sure, if the world is intelligently designed there yet remains the pivotal question: how did it get that way? And at this point there comes a forking of the way into two available routes, namely: by *natural* means or by *super-* or *supranatural* means. There is nothing about intelligent design as such that constrains one route or the other. Intelligent design does not require or presuppose an intelligent designer any more than an oddly designed reality would require an odd designer. A naturally emerging object is not made into an artifact by its possession of a feature whose artifice *might also* produce. Again, being intelligently designed no more demands an intelligent designer than saying it is harmoniously arranged requires a harmonious arranger or saying it is spatially extended requires a spatial extender.

Against this background it would appear that there is thus nothing mystical about a revivified neo-Platonism. It is strictly geared to nature's modus operandi. Insofar as teleology is at work, it is a naturalistic teleology.

Here many participants in the debates about intelligent design get things badly confused. Deeply immersed in a theism-antipathetic *odium theologicum* they think that divine creation is the only pathway to intelligent design and thereby feel impelled to reject the idea of an intelligently designed universe in order to keep God out of it. They think that intelligent design can only come to realization through the intermediation of an intelligently designing creator. But this view sees matters askew. A perfectly natural impetus to harmonious co-ordination could perfectly well fit in an intelligently designed result. And so could the natural selection inherent in some macroevolutionary process.

The hypothetical and conditional character of the present line of reasoning must be acknowledged. It does no more than maintain the purely conditional thesis that *if* intelligent creatures are going to emerge in the world by evolutionary processes, *then* the world must be ratiophilic, so to speak—that is, user-friendly for rational intelligences. It is not, of course, being argued that the world must contain intelligent beings by virtue of some sort of transcendental necessity. Rather, a conditional situation—if intelligence-containing then intelligible—is quite sufficient for present purposes. For the question at hand is why we intelligent creatures present on the world's stage should be able to understand its operations in significant measure. And the conditional story described above fully suffices to accomplish this particular job in view of linking evolution and intelligent design.

Derailing Wastage as an Objection to Evolved Design

To be sure there can be objections. One of them runs as follows: "Is evolution by variation and survivalist selection not an enormously wasteful mode of operation? And is it not cumbersome and much too slow? Does this sort of moving not rule intelligence out of it?"

Not really. For where the objector complains of *wastage* here, a more generous spirit might see a Leibnizian principle of fertility at work that gives a wide variety of life forms their chance for a moment in the limelight. (Perhaps the objector wouldn't think much of being a dinosaur, but then many are the small children who wouldn't agree.) Anyway, perhaps it is better to be a microbe than to be a "Wasn't that just Isn't"—to invoke Dr. Seuss. Or again, one person's waste is another's fertility—to invoke Leibniz.

But what of all that suffering that follows to the lot of organic existence? Perhaps it is just collateral damage in the cosmic struggle towards intelligent life. But this is neither the place nor the time for producing a theodicy and addressing the theological problem of evil. The salient point is simply that the wastage objection is not automatically telling and that various lines of reply are available to deflect its impact.

Now, on to the charge of slowness. Surely the proper response to the lethargy objection is to ask: what's the rush? In relation to a virtually infinite vastness of time, any finite initial timespan is but an instant.

Of course there must be time enough for evolutionary processes to work out. There must be *sufficiency*. But nothing patent is achieved by *minimality* unless there is some mysterious collective reason why this particular benefit—an economy of time—should be prioritized over other desiderata such as variety, fertility, or the like.

Intelligent Design Does Not Require Absolute Perfection

Yet another objection arises along the following lines: "Does not reality's all too evident imperfection constitute a decisive roadblock to intelligent design? For if optimal alternatives were always realized, would not the world be altogether perfect in every regard?"

By no means! After all, the best achievable result for a whole will, in various realistic conditions, require a less than perfect outcome for the parts. A game with multiple participants cannot be won by every one of them. A society of many members cannot put each of them at the top of the heap. In an engaging and suspenseful plot, things cannot go with unalloyed smoothness for every character.

Moreover, there are generally multiple parameters of positivity that function competitively so that some can only be enhanced at the cost of others—even as to make a car speedier we must sacrifice operating cost.

With an automobile, the parameters of merit clearly includes such factors as speed, reliability, repair infrequency, safety, operating economy, aesthetic appearance, road handling ability. But in actual practice such features are interrelated. It is unavoidable that they trade off against one another: more of A means less of B. It would be ridiculous to have a super-safe car with a maximum speed of two miles per hour. It would be ridiculous to have a car that is inexpensive to operate but spends three-fourths of the time in a repair shop. Invariably, perfection—an all-at-once maximization of every value dimension—is inherently unrealizable because of the inherent interaction of evaluative parameters. In designing a car you cannot maximize both safety and economy of operation, and analogously, the world is not, and cannot possibly be, absolutely perfect—perfect in *every* respect—because this sort of absolute perfection is in principle impossible.

In the context of multiple and potentially competing parameters of merit, the idea of an all-at-once maximization has to give way to an on-balance optimization.

The fact of it is that every object of value will have a *plurality* of evaluative features, some of which will in some respects stand in conflict. Where interest rots in complexity, we sacrifice simplicity; where beauty lies in simplicity we sacrifice complexity. And this being so, *absolute* perfection becomes, in principle, infeasible. For what we have here is a relation of competition and tradeoff among modes of merit akin to the complementary relation of quantum physics. The holistic and systemic optimality of a complex whole will require some of its constituent comportments to pay a price. They will fall short of what they would be if abstractly considered in detached iso-lation. This suffices to sideline the objection: "If intelligent design prevails, why isn't the world absolutely perfect?"

The present discussion has argued that evolution is not at odds with intelligent design, because the efficiency tropism inherent in the mo-dus operandi of evolutionary development actually renders it likely in an intelligently designed product. Accordingly, evolution should not be seen as the antithesis of intelligent design. Nor is it inimical to a theology of an intelligent designer. In arranging for a developmental pathway to an intelligently designed world, a benign creator could well opt for an evolutionary process. So in the end, evolution and intelligent design need not be seen as antagonistic.

In closing it must be stressed that noophelia can be entirely natu-ralistic, but it is nevertheless altogether congenial to theism. To be sure, there is no reason of necessity why a universe that is intelli-gently designed as user-friendly for intelligent beings must be the result of the agency of an intelligent being any more than a universe that is clumsily designed for accommodating clumsy beings would have to be the creative product of a clumsy being. But while this is so, such a universe is altogether harmonious to theistic cosmogony. After all, an intelligently construed universe is altogether consonant with a cosmogony of divine creation. And so: *noophelia is not only compatible with but actually congenial to theism.* After all, one can-not but think that the well-being of its intelligent creatures will rank high in the value scheme of a benign creator. As should really be the case in general, approaches based on the study of nature and the reflections of theology can here be brought into alignment.[4]

6

Fallacies Regarding Free Will

Philosophical controversy regarding the freedom of the will has been astir since the dawn of the subject. The freedom at issue calls for an agent's being in conscious control of what they do in ways that are at odds with the prospect that their thoughts and intentions could be bypassed in an adequate explanation of their actions. The contradictory position—determinism—holds instead that agent control is an illusion and that the processes of nature settle matters of action without regard to the substance of the agent's mental operations.

Despite the elaborate controversies that have prevailed on this topic over the centuries, several fallacies and flaws of thought have been able to gain a tenacious and seemingly permanent hold on the way in which people address the issues. It is constructive to consider some salient examples.

Fallacy Number One

The first fallacy inheres in an idea that Daniel Dennett has articulated as follows:

If determinism is true, then our every deed and decision is the inexorable outcome, it seems, of the sum of physical forces acting at the moment; which in turn is the inexorable outcome of the forces acting an instant before, *and so on to the beginning of time*. . . . [Thus]—If determinism is true, then our acts are the consequences of the laws of nature and events in the remote past. But it is not up to us what went on before we were born, and neither is it up to us what the laws of nature are. Therefore the consequences of these things (including our present acts) are not up to us.[1]

It is exactly in this transit from "*and so on*" to "*the beginning of time*" that constitutes what I shall call the Zenonic fallacy. It overlooks the prospect of backwards *convergence* as illustrated in the following diagram:

Here t_{i+1} stands halfway between t_i and X.

Consider an occurrence O at t_0, putatively the product of a free decision at X. To explain it in terms of what precedes, we certainly do not need to go back to "the beginning of time."

The failing at issue here is substantially that of Zeno's notorious paradox of Achilles and the tortoise. Both alike involve a fallacy in overlooking the circumstance that, thanks to convergence, an infinity of steps can be taken in a finite distance, provided merely that the steps get progressively shorter. Once it is granted that, even if a cause must precede its effect, there is no specificative timespan, however small, by which it need do so, the causal regression argument against free will looses all of its traction.

With Zeno, Achilles never catches the tortoise because his progress must go on and on before the endpoint is reached. In the present reasoning, explanation will never reach an initiating choice point because the regress goes on and on. But in both cases, the idea of a convergence that terminated the infinite process at issue after a finite timespan is simply ignored.

Such a perspective leaves the principle of causality wholly compatible with freedom because that act and all its causal antecedents remain causally explicable.

Fallacy Number Two

Human choices are generally predictable and predictability is at odds with free will.

The reality of it is that predictability is simply no problem. If I offer you the choice between a hundred dollar bill and a needless root canal operation, there is no difficulty in predicting which you will choose. But your choice is nevertheless perfectly free.

What matters for freedom is not predictability as such, but rather the basis of prediction. If and when the prediction rests on the agent's tastes, dispositions, preferences, and so forth, then that decision is free.

"But we do not choose our tastes, dispositions, and so on." Perfectly true, but also quite beside the point. The objection rests on an erroneous premise: "Choices are free only if their motives are freely chosen." But this requirement is inappropriate and immaterial. For by their very nature, motives, tastes, and so forth are not themselves objects of choice at all.

Nor are they somehow forced on the agent by constituents from without. They are not externally *imposed*, they are internally constituted in the agent—a part of what makes an agent into the individual he or she is. They are components of their very nature.

Fallacy Number Three

If all events are explicable in the order of natural causality, then so are all of those supposedly free decision of agents. This means that the law of causality leaves no room for agent causality and thus no room for free will.

To avoid this fallacy we must draw a couple of basic distinctions. The first and most crucial distinction here is that between two sorts of occurrences: events and eventuations. Events are occurrences that form part of nature's processuality. They are happenings on the world's spatiotemporal stage. So they transpire over time: they have a finite lifespan and their time of existence always occupies an open interval.

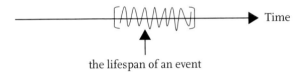

the lifespan of an event

Eventuations, by contrast, are not parts of nature's processuality but terminating points within it. They are temporally punctiform and lack duration. They mark the beginnings and endings of events.

Now all human *acts* (all actions and activities) are event-like. They occupy time. But the junctures of resolution that mark the completion of a process of choice and decision are not events. Such completions are not actually processual doings, but rather are mere junctures of passage—transitions that mark the beginnings and endings of events. Looking for something is an activity, but actually finding it is not. (There is no present continuous here. One can be engaged in looking but not in finding.) Listening to someone is an activity, but hearing what they say is not. Activities are events, terminations and completions are not. The running of a race is an event (as are its various parts, such as running the first half of the race). However, *finishing* the race is an eventuation. Such eventuations are endings or culminations. One can ask, "How long did he take him to *run* the race?" but not "How long did he take to *start* the race?" And even as the race ends when it is won (or lost), so the task ends exactly at the moment when it is completed (or abandoned). Finishing is thus an eventuation, and accordingly, the finishing point of a race, instead of being the last instant of the race, is the first instant at which the race is no longer in progress. And this is also the case with the decisions and choices that terminate a course of deliberations.

Eventuations, so understood, are not parts of nature's processual flow, since *parts* of processes are always processes themselves. Rather, eventuations—the beginnings and endings—belong to the machinery of conceptualization that minds impose on nature: instrumentalities of descriptive convenience that do not correspond to anything enjoying independent existence in the real world. Like the North Pole or the equator they are not real items existing physically in nature, but rather thought instrumentalities projected into reality by minds proceeding in the interests of description and examination.

Deliberations, so regarded, are seen as events—as processes that occur over open-ended intervals of time and culminate in decisions as eventuations. But these culminations are end points. And this means that there will always be an interval of time between a decision and any *subsequent* action—an interval able to accommodate intervening events to serve as causal explainers of that decision/consequent action. *Since there is no such thing as a next time subsequent to a point of decision, there will always be room for squeezing in further events before any particular decision/subsequent event.*

The prospect of determination by events is thus ever present. And analogously, there is not a first decision-succeeding event that excludes the prospect of a prior occurrence-explaining event. This is critical for the present positions regarding the causal explainability of actions.

Freedom of decision accordingly does not impede causal explicability. However, what one has in the wake of a free decision is a phenomenon that might be characterized as *causal compression*. Every event that ensues from that decision can be accounted for causally—but only with reference to occurrences during the immediately preceding but decision-subsequent timespan, whose duration converges to zero as the point of decision is approached.

In sum: once we duly distinguish events from eventuations we can regard all action (as events) to be causally explicable in terms of what precedes. Free will becomes reconciled to the causal explicability of actions. A free decision inaugurates a series of events each of which is fully explicable and determinate on the order of natu-

Display 6.1. Timing Issues

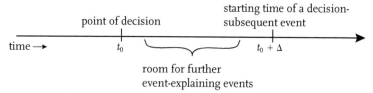

Note: There is no next point after a given point and the starting point of the *subsequent* interval.

ral causality. But this is something that is true of all those decision-subsequent events and does not hold for that free decision itself.

Thus while overt actions (and thereby also those that are free) will always in principle admit of a *causal* explanation, this will not be so with decisions and choices. And thereby hangs a lesson. Modern science is a good deal better at explaining natural phenomena than at explaining psychological phenomena. It is thus not surprising that scientistically inclined determinists prefer addressing free agency rather than free decision. But of course freedom of the will pivots fundamentally on the latter issue, a free action being one that emerges—however deterministically—from a free choice or decision.

Fallacy Number Four

Since predetermination is incompatible with free will, so is the determination of a decision's outcome by the agent's own decision-engendering deliberations.

This objection overlooks an important distinction, namely that between *pre-determination* and what might be called *precedence determination*. The former calls for predictability as of some antecedent time; the latter involves no such thing. This crucial difference is illustrated by the following diagram.

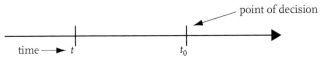

With *predetermination* what happens at t_0 is determined by (that is, law-deducible from) that which happens at some earlier time, t. Already at this earlier time the decision becomes settled: a foregone conclusion that is reached in advance of the fact. Some earlier state of affairs renders what occurs at the time causally inevitable. With precedence determination, by contrast, what happens at t_0 is also determined by what goes before—but only by *everything* that happens from some earlier time t up to but not including t_0.[2] Both alike are modes of determination by earlier history. But unlike the former, the latter *requires an infinite amount of input information* that is of course never available. What we thus have in this latter case is a mode of antecedence determination that does not give rise to predictability but is in fact incompatible with it.

Such precedence determination can and should be contemplated in relation to free decisions and choices: a determination by the concluding phase of the course of the agent's deliberation that eventuates in the decision or choice at issue.

Predetermination means that the outcome becomes a foregone conclusion at some antecedent time. The entire matter becomes settled in advance of the fact. This is indeed incompatible with free will because it deprives the agent of the power to change his mind. There is some time in advance of the point of decision when the whole matter becomes settled.

The events that constitute a course of deliberation antecedent to a decision or choice so function as to determine the outcome, *it is only the endgame, the final, concluding phase that is decisive.*

Precedence determination, by contrast, means that the final phase of the deliberation is decisive. Only the entire course of the agent's thinking from *some* earlier point up to *but not including* the point of decision suffices to settle the issue. The outcome is never settled in advance—it isn't over "until the fat lady sings." And it should be clear that this sort of antecedent determination geared to the unfolding course of deliberation in its final phase is nowise at odds with freedom of the will.

The situation of a free choice among alternatives is thus associated with the following sort of picture regarding the situation at issue.

Consider, by way of example, a course of deliberation for deciding among three alternatives, A, B, and C, with the decision ultimately arrived at in favor of C at time t_0, the "point of decision." At every time t before t_0 there are three possible outcomes, A, B, and C, whose probabilities at any given time prior to t_0 share a band of width 1 overall, as per display 6.2.

Throughout the course of deliberation these probabilities may wobble across the probability band, but in the end, they must converge in a way that at t_0 gives the whole probability to one outcome alone. But at any time prior to t_0 there is a nonzero probability that

Display 6.2. An Example of Deliberating and Probability Dynamics

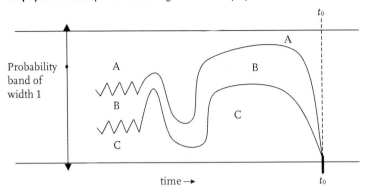

any of the three outcomes will result—at no anterior time is the outcome a foregone conclusion. The endgame is never definitively settled before the end is reached: only at the very end (at t_0) is there a "probability collapse" into 1 and 0's. Until the issue is "fully decided," there is a nonzero probability of the agent's making a choice different from the one that ultimately eventuated. As the "point of decision" is reached it becomes more and more likely how the issue will resolve itself. But there are no guarantees. At no time before that point of decision is there a "point of no return" where the resolution becomes a foregone conclusion.

So once again a distinction comes upon the scene to save the day. The objection in view is fallacious because it overlooks the crucial distinction between the two very different modes of "determination by what precedes" represented respectively by pre-determination and precedence determination of the sort just described.

And one other point is important here. The first question to ask of any mode of determinism is determination *by what?* By matters outside the agent's range of motivation is one thing. But by the agent's own deliberations—by the manifold of inclination that encompasses his wants, wishes, aims, and choices is something else again. After all, determination of decision outcomes by the agent's thoughts is surely a requisite of free will rather than an obstacle to it.

Fallacy Number Five

An act can be free only if its productive source is located in the thoughts and deliberations of the agent. But this is never the case because the tight linkage of mind activity to brain activity means that the thoughts and deliberations of the agent's mind are always rooted in and explicable through the processes at work in the agent's brain.

To see what is amiss here consider the fact that two parameters are lockstep coordinated does not settle—or even address—the issue of which one has processual initiative.

All of those myriad illustrations of a correlation between thought and brain activity are simply immaterial to the issue of who is in charge. Either direction remains possible. For the determinist, to be sure, agents are productively inert—what they do is always the product of what happens to them: they simply provide the stage on which the causality of nature performs its drama. The voluntarist, by contrast, sees intelligent agents as productively active participants in the drama of the world's physical processuality. And the reality of it is that mind-brain correlation cannot effectively be used against him. It is simply fallacious to think that the intimate linkage between brain activity and thought puts the brain in charge of the mind.

With such an approach, the brain/mind is seen as an emergently evolved dual-aspect organization whose two interlinked domains permit the impetus for change to lie sometimes on the one side and sometimes on the other side. For the *direction* of determination so far remains open. Given these interlocked variables, the question of the dependent versus the independent status is wholly open, and the question of *initiative* is unresolved. And the fact that the mind and brain sail in the same boat is no reason why the mind cannot occasionally seize the tiller. What is at issue is a partnership of *coordination,* not a state of inflexible master-servant *subordination.* In particular situations, the initiative can lie on one side or the other— all depending.

But all depending on what? How does it get decided where the initiative lies? Well—think of the pulley situation. When the cube rises, is this because someone is pushing up on it or because a bird has alighted on the sphere? The system itself taken in isolation will not answer this for you, but the wider context—the overall causality synoptic and dynamic context—will decide where the initiative lies. It is all a matter of where the activity starts and what stands at the end of the causal line. And the free will situation is much the same. When I read, the mind responds to the body; when I write, the body responds to the mind.

Fallacy Number Six

If the acts of an agent are anywise determined—if they are somehow, that is, anywise necessitated—then they cannot possibly qualify as free.

Both Aristotle and the Stoics sought to reconcile the volitional freedom they deemed requisite for morality with the determinism they saw operative in the circumstance that character dictates decisions. To accomplish this without adopting the Platonic myth of character selection, they maintained that what would impede freedom is not determination as such but only *exogenous* determination rooted in factors outside the agent's self-produced motivations. The crux of freedom, so viewed, is not indetermination but autodetermination—determination effected by the agent's agency itself—*sua sponite* as the medievals put it.

With such a compatibilist view, the crux of the matter is not whether or not there is determinism—it is conceded that there indeed is, albeit of the agent-internal variety. The crux is whether there is an agent-external determinism—a determinism where all reference to the agent and their motivations can be out of consideration in matters of explanation. The issue of freedom does not turn on the *that* of determination, but on its *how*, its procedural mechanisms. For as long as those deliberative factors are critical for determination, the basis for freedom is secured.

Thus, we have a distinction here between endogenous (agent-internal) and exogenous (agent-external) determination. Clearly if that determination is effected without reference to the agent by forces and factors above and beyond his control by thought, then we can hardly characterize that agent as free. But if those determinative factors are agent-internal, if they are a matter of the agent's own plans and projects, his own wishes, desires, and purposes, then the deliberation of the values of decisions and choices nowise stands in the way of the agent's freedom. A choice or decision that was not the natural and inevitable outcome of the agent's motivations could hardly qualify as a free decision.

And so freedom of the will is nowise at odds with the principle of causality as long as the locus of causal determination is located in the thought process of the agent—that is, as long as causal determination is canalized through the mediation of the choices and decisions emergent from his deliberations. And there is consequently no opposition between freedom and causal determination as long as that determination is effected by what transpires in the principle of agents and the matter is one of agent causality.[3]

In sum, to set free will at odds with determinacy is fundamentally fallacious because it rides roughshod over the crucial distinction— that between the agent-external causality of impersonal events and the agent-internal causality that involves deliberative thought.

Fallacy Number Seven

Free will is mysterious and supranatural. For it requires a suspension of disbelief regarding the standard view of natural occurrence subject to the principle of causality.

Along these lines one recent writer complains:[4]

Agent causation is a frankly mysterious doctrine, positing something unparalleled by anything we discover in the causal processes of chemical reactionism, nuclear fission and fusion, magnetic attraction, hurricanes, volcanoes, or such biological processes as metabolism, growth, immune reactions, and photosynthesis. Is there such a thing? When libertarians insist that there must be, they [build upon sand].[5]

But this sort of complaint is deeply problematic.

Free will, properly regarded, hinges on the capacity of the mind to seize the initiative in effecting changes in the developmental course of mind-brain coordinated occurrence. Need this, or *should* this, be seen as something mysterious and supranatural?

With the evolution of minds upon the world stage, various capacities and capabilities come upon the scene emergently, adding new sorts of operations to the repertoire of mammalian operations—remembering past occurrences, for example, or imagining future ones. And one of these developmental innovations is the capacity of the mind to take the initiative in effecting change in the setting of the mind from coordinate developments.

Now the explanatory rationale for this innovation is substantially the same as that for any other sort of evolution-emergent capability, namely that it contributes profitability to the business of natural selection. There is nothing mysterious or supranatural about it.

And so this present fallacy rests on a failure of imagination. It is predicated in an inability to actualize that with the evolution of intelligent agents there arises the prospect of intelligence-guided agency determined through the deliberations of these intelligent agents.

Fallacy Number Eight

Down the corridors of time have echoed the words of Spinoza:

> Men believe that they are free, precisely because they are conscious of their volitions and decisions, and think not in the slightest about the causes that dispose them to those appetites and volitions, since they are unknown to them.[6]

Apparently Spinoza thought (perhaps with Freud) that action is only genuinely free when it is activated entirely by recognized and rationally evaluated and approved motives. But this simply confounds *free* with *rational* agency. As long as the agent acts on his own motives—without external duress or manipulation—his action is free in the standard (rather than rationalistically reconfigured) sense of the term. Motivation as such does not impede freedom—be it rationally grounded or not. Our motives, however inappropriate and ill-advised they may be and however little understood in terms of their psychogenesis, do not *constrain* our will externally but are the very core of its expression.

A will that is responsive to an agent's motivation is thereby free and it matters not how compelling that motive may be in relation to the resolution at issue.[7] After all, a person's nature is manifested in his or her decisions and finds its overt expression realized in that person. His or her decisions are nothing but the overt manifestation of an inner motivational nature. It is through decisions and consequent actions that people display what they actually are.

Consider this situation. I ask someone to pick a number from one to six. They select six. I suspected as much: their past behavior indicates a preference for larger numbers over smaller and for evens over odds. So their choice was not entirely random. Does that make it unfree? Not at all! It was nowise forced or constrained. Those number preferences were not external pressures that restricted freedom: on the contrary they paved the way to self-expression. It would be folly to see freedom as antithetical to motivation. Quite to the contrary! Volitional freedom is a freedom to indulge one's motivations.

To "free" the will from obeisance to the agent's aims and motives, needs and wants, desires and goals, likes and values, personality and disposition is not to liberate it, but to make it into something that is not just useless but even counterproductive. What rational agent would want to be harnessed to the decision-effecting instrumentality that left his motivations by the wayside? A will detached from the agent's motives would surely not qualify as *his*! It is a rogue will, not a personal one.

Fallacy Number Nine

The very idea of free will is antithetical to science. Free will is something occult that cannot possibly be naturalized.

It is—or should be—hard to work up much sympathy to this objection. For if free will exists—if *Homo sapiens* can indeed make free choices and decisions—then this of course has to be part of the natural order of things. So if we indeed are free then this has to be so for roughly the same reason that we are intelligent—that is, because evolution works things out that way.

What lies at the heart and core of free will is, up to the last moment, thought control by a rational agent of their deliberation-produced choices and decisions in the light of their ongoing updated information and evaluation. To see that such a capacity is of advantage in matters of survival is not a matter of rocket science.

The objection at issue is thus fallacious in that it rests in the inappropriate presupposition that free will has to be something super- or preternatural. If there is free will, it will have to be an aspect of how naturally evolved beings operate on nature's stage. The fact that we humans get here by evolution does not mean that we cannot make free decisions anymore than it does not mean that we cannot solve calculus problems or play chess. There simply is no decisive reason for denying that just as evolution is capable of having intelligent beings evolve, so it is capable of having intelligent agents evolve—creatures whose actions are the product of thought-determined decisions.

But enough! We have now looked at nine fallacious arguments against freedom of the will, and the list could easily be continued. But the overall lesson should already be clear. Time and again a misconception arises that can be overcome by drawing appropriate distinctions whose heed makes for a more viable construal of how freedom of the will—if such there is—should be taken to work. So at each stage there is some further clarification of what free will involves. There gradually emerges from the fog an increasingly clear view that what is at issue here is the capacity of intelligent beings to resolve matters of choice and decision through a process of deliberation on the basis of beliefs and desires that allows for ongoing updates and up to the bitter end revisability.

And so while these present considerations do not establish that the will is free, nevertheless they provide for a dialectic of the following structure:

> The general tenor of everyday experience leads people to think of themselves as free agents who control their decisions and actions. In the face of the pro-presumption that this circumstance establishes, it will take a strong argument to the contrary to defeat it. But the flaws and fallacies one encounters throughout the range of the standard determinist arguments serve to indicate that the opposition simply lacks the requisite strength to prevail.

Properly understood, freedom of the will should not be at odds with our knowledge about how things work in the world. A viable theory of free will should—nay, must—proceed on a naturalistic basis. And the idea that this is infeasible appears to be, by all the available indications, based on an incorrect and fallacious view of what freedom of the will is all about.

7

Mind and Matter

A Two-Sided Coin

For centuries, issues of mind-matter interaction have preoccupied philosophers, and recently modern science has added fuel to the fire. But unfortunately, the interpretation of most science-inspired theorizing about mind-matter interaction is hopelessly muddied through misconstruing brain activity and the physiological gearing of the body to mental thought, that the latter is somehow governed and determined by the machinations of the former. Granted, there is a linkage with these two resources operating in unison with the result of what one recent writer refers to as:

> The Correlation Thesis . . . to the effect that there exists for each discriminable conscious state or occurrence [in the *mind* of an agent] a theoretically discernable [characteristically coordinate] brain correlate.[1]

For even if we grant such a rigid, lockstep coordination, there still remains the question of who is in charge of a given transaction? Who commands and who follows? Which is the dependent and which the independent variable? Clearly, the tighter the coordination the more pressing this questions becomes. Unison of operation will not as such establish primacy of control. And this critical point is almost universally overlooked. For causation is potentially a two-way street here. Changes in psychological states carry changes in cerebral physiology in their wake: when the mind frets, the brain buzzes. And conversely, changes in brain states carry changes in mind states in their wake. And the coordination of mind and matter—however tight—does not put matter into the driver's seat. One can think of mental activity as a matter of the mind's awareness of what the brain is doing. And conversely, one can think of brain activity as the brain's response to or reflection of what the mind is doing. But there is no reason to think of either of these alternatives as an inevitable arrangement, excluding the prospect that sometimes the balance tilts one way or another.

In the end, any adequate mind/body theory must accommodate two facts of common experience:

1. The mind responds to bodily changes (drugs, fatigue, anesthetics, and so on).

2. The body responds to many of the mind's demands (to stand up, walk about, hold one's breath, and so forth).

Now consider in this light the following oft-maintained contention:

An act can be free only if its productive source is located in the thoughts and deliberations of the agent. But this is never the case because the tight linkage of mind activity to brain activity means that the thoughts and deliberations of the agent's mind are always rooted in and explicable through the processes at work in the agent's brain.

To see what is amiss here, think of the classic freshman physics setup of a gas-containing, cylindrical chamber closed off by a piston at one end. The temperature inside the chamber is coordinated in lockstep coordinate with the distance of the piston wall from the fixed wall: when the piston moves the temperature changes correspondingly, and conversely, when temperature changes are induced the piston moves correspondingly. But this condition of functional lockstep correlation leaves the issue of initiative wholly open: one may either be changing the temperature by moving the piston or moving the piston by changing the temperature. Thus lockstep coordination as such does not settle the question of the direction of determination, which of the coordinated variables is free and which is dependent. The fact that two parameters are lockstep coordinated does not determine—or even address—the issue of processual initiative.

Again, consider a teeter-totter or, alternatively, a pulley arrangement:

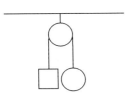 Here, the upward or downward motion of the one weight is inseparably tied to the corresponding motion of the other.

Lockstep coordination leaves totally open the issue of where the initiative to change actually lies. And this illustrates the larger point: however tight and rigid the functional coordination between two interactive agencies—such as mind and brain—may be, the issue of initiative and change-inauguration is something that yet remains entirely open and unaddressed. Mark Twain's tendentious question, "When the body is drunk, does the mind stay sober?" is perfectly appropriate. But then the reverse question, "When the mind panics does the body remain calm?" is no less telling.

The Issue of Initiative

As previously mentioned, the connection between thought and brain activity is simply immaterial to the issue of who is in charge. For what is involved cannot settle the question of whether the mind responds passively to brain-state changes, or whether it actively uses the brain for its own ends.

Consider the following argument: "Our mental performances correspond to physico-mental processes in the brain, which as such answer to nature's laws of cause and effect. Ergo those fundamental processes of inert nature encompass the realm of thought as well." There is a deep flaw in this reasoning—a flaw that lies in a failure to realize that correspondence and correlation do not settle the issue of initiative. Irrespective of how tightly the operations of the mind are connected with those of the brain, this does not establish—or even engage—the issue of initiation, the question of whether it is the mind or brain that is, what Moritz Schlick called, the "original instigator."[2]

There is good reason to see the mind-brain interlinkage in much the same instigating terms. And here too, the linkage as such does not set a fixed direction to the initiative and control of changes. Anger the individual and characteristic patterns of brain activities will ensue; create a characteristic pattern of activity in the brain (say by electrical stimulus), and the person will respond with anger. Yes, there indeed is a tight correlation, but productivity functions along a two-way street. The correlation of the mind and brain is no more an obstacle to thought-initiated physical responses than it is an obstacle to the evocation through thought the responses of physical stimuli. My annoyance at the pin-prick is a triumph of matter over mind; my extraction of the pin a triumph of mind over matter.[3]

When my finger wiggles because I decide to move it, for the sake of illustration, then the mind side of the mind/brain configuration sets the brain side into motion. By contrast, when I hear the alarm clock ring, it is the brain side of the mind/brain configuration that alerts the mind side to a wake-up call. The mind/brain amalgamation leaves the issue of the *direction* of motivation—be it brain-initiated mind receptivity or mind-inaugurated brain responsiveness—open to further resolution. With agent causation originating in the mind, the agent is active; with physical considerations originating in the brain, the agent is passive. Both are perfectly possible. And each happens some of the time with neither enjoying a monopoly.

Mind clearly cannot do the work of matter: it cannot on its own produce snow or ripen tomatoes. Nor, it would seem, can matter do the work of mind: it cannot read books or solve crosswords. And yet the two are clearly connected. When the mind decides to raise the hand, that hand moves. And on the other side there is Mark Twain's question introduced above. Clearly, there is *interaction* here.

Mind-body coordination does not, as such, endow the brain with an invariable initiative, but this is not the place to articulate a full-scale philosophy of mind. The extensive detail of mind-brain coordination will not preoccupy us here.[4] All that is requisite for present purposes is that there is a tight linkage of mind-brain coordination, and that when a state change occurs in this context the initiative for it can lie on either side. We need not here enter into detail at a level that transcends these rudimentary basics.

That said, it must be acknowledged that the conception of a mind-brain partnership of coordination in which a process of a change in psychophysical states can be initiated on either side is critically important in the present context. For it opens the way to seeing free decisions as a crucial, productive contribution of the mind to the world's panoply of occurrence.

A Salient Duality

What we have with mind-body coordination is not a mysteriously imposed preestablished harmony, but an internally assured coestablished alignment—a dual-aspect account if you will. Even as what is for the paper a squiggle of ink is for the reader a meaningful word, so one selfsame psychophysical process is for the brain a *signal* (a causal stimulus) and for the mind a *sign* (a unit of meaning). Or again, one selfsame process, the ringing of the dinner bell, has one sort of significance ever-obvious of the guests and another for their mind-set. Such analogies, while imperfect, should help to convey the general idea of phenomena that have an inherent duality. In our piston example above, the mode of the piston manifests itself in changes of the chamber area and heat-wise in a change of temperature.

That piston setup is a thermodynamic engine; the mind is a hermeneutical engine. For only a mind can operate the symbolic processes that transform stimuli into meanings. Those physical inclinations are the *occasion* and perhaps even in some sense the *productive cause* of the interpretations at issue, but they are not the *bearers* of its substantive meaning content. For that requires a very different level of understanding and a very different framework of conceptualization.

All the same, the mind no more functions independently of the brain than the expressive mood of the visage can smile Cheshire cat-like without the physical face. And yet, that physical face can achieve no expression in the absence of there being a psychological mood to express.

Rigid materialism sees mental action as a systemically subordinate response to the functioning of matter. Rigid idealism sees matter as somehow engendered through the productive activity of mind. But more realistic than either is a theory of mind-matter coordination that sees the two as reciprocally conjoined.

With any system in which there are functionally coordinated factors (be they temperature/pressure or supply/demand or whatever) a change in the one can engender change in the other. What we have here, then, is a situation of coordination and reciprocity rather than a case of unidirectional dominance/subordination. Being anxious can make the pulse race; but then again, sensing one's pulse racing can induce anxiety. The interconnection and interaction of mind and body can work both ways. Granted, where the brain is dead the mind no longer works. But then as long as the mind is working the healthy brain responds. Thought is not an epiphenomenon to physical processes but a co-phenomenon coordinate with certain ones among them. Thinking is not something the brain does: it is done by a mind that uses the brain as *its* instrument.

When thought leads to action it is not that two different *kinds* of causality are at work. The causality of agency (thought control) and the causality of nature (brain control) are two sides of the same coin as it were, two inseparably conjoined aspects of one comprehensive causal process. The changes at issue flow from one unified sort of "causality." It is just that the actuating impetus to those changes in the one case lies at the pole of thought processes and in the other case at the pole of brain processes. And so when the mind has the initiative, the brain does not *react* but rather *responds*—and the converse is true as well. So strictly speaking, rather than causality, influence is at work. After all, a suggestion can induce or occasion an idea in someone's mind without "producing" it in some manufacturing analogous sense of the term.

On the issue of who is in charge, the mind or brain, thought or matter, traditional philosophizing has almost always taken an all-or-nothing approach. Materialistic determinists from classical atomism to the time of Hobbes, La Mettrie, and Laplace put matter in charge; idealists from Socrates to Berkeley and Lotze put the mind in charge.[5] For some reason the commonsense idea that in some transactions the one is in control and in others the other had little appeal for philosophy's endless succession of absolutists. But in the end, there is really no reason to opt for an all-or-nothing resolution.

Mind-Brain Interaction Works by Coordination, Not by Causality

With mind-brain coordination in place, mind as well as matter can seize the initiative with respect to human action so that we can act in the mode of agent causality, while nevertheless all human actions can be explained via natural causality. And so, we confront Kant's paradox of reconciling the two modes of causality.[6]

But how, with such a view, does mind come to exercise physical causality? When I mentally decide to wiggle my fingers a few seconds hence for the sake of an example, how is it that my body responds to this purely mental transaction? The answer is that it doesn't because no "purely mental" transaction is at issue. Thought always has its correlative in the domain of brain psychology.[7] And so, an individual's so-called purely mental intention is not really *purely* mental at all, because it is coordinate with a mind-brain amalgamating, psychophysiological intention state. And the physical cause of that wiggling response is not something "purely mental" but the physical side of that amalgam.

What actually occurs in such transactions is less a matter of causality than of coordination. In his classic paper of 1934, Dickinson Miller saw the matter quite clearly:

> [In choosing or deciding] the mental process is paralleled in the brain by a physical process. The whole [two-sided] psychophysical occurrence would then be the cause of what followed, and the psychic side of it—the mental struggle proper—a concause or side of the [overall, two-sided] cause. Tomorrow's configuration of matter [that is, the physical result of an action] will [then] have been brought about by a material [physical] process with which the mental process was inseparably conjoined.[8]

When an agent acts there is no need to dream up a Cartesian category or a transcending impetus of thought upon matter. The material eventuations are produced materially, by the physical side of the two-sided mind-matter amalgam at issue in psychophysical processes. And the same applies to thought processes. Each component functions in its own order, but the coordinate linkage of the two move in lockstep, thus automatically answering Mark Twain's question introduced earlier, "When the body is drunk, does the mind stay sober?" The one thing this account leaves out—and it is a crucial omission—is the key, recurring point that the actuating *initiative* for change can lie on either side.

But what could account for the fact that on this occasion the initiative lies with the mind and on that occasion it lies with the brain? Here we need to look to the temporal context of occurrence in its more comprehensive gestalt. If what I do comes in response to drink or drugs, then it is clearly the brain that is in charge. On the other hand if it is a matter of careful deliberation and a painstaking weighing of alternatives, then it is clearly the mind that is in charge. It all depends on the structure of occurrence subject to the same sort of contextual analysis that is at issue with the discrimination between dependent and independent parameters in physical process situations. For here as elsewhere, the wider context of occurrence can settle the question of productive priority and initiative.

The causal deliberations of the ancient Greeks were predicated on the idea that only like can cause like. The idea that factors that are as different *conceptually* as night and day could nevertheless influence one another *causally* was anathema to them. But the reality of it stands otherwise. Motion creates heat via friction; sounds engender salivation by Pavlovian conditioning. Yet not only was this consideration rejected by the Greeks, but it continued to exert influence as late as Descartes, who continued with his Chinese wall separation of mind from matter. However, the revolution in causal thinking launched by David Hume changed all that. The idea of cross category causation no longer seems all that odd to us. And we nowadays do not—or should not—see any inherent impossibility that in the order of causal production physical processes should engender mental responses—or the other way around.[9]

In the end then, regardless of how tight the correlation of mind and matter may be, there is no ground for construing this circumstance as precluding the efficacy of the mind in effecting change. Indeed, there is no reason to refrain from maintaining that it is sometimes the mind, rather than matter that affords the independent variable that takes the initiative in the inauguration of change. The tighter the interrelatedness of the brain and matter, then the ampler the prospects become for transactions where the mind has the initiative. It is not functional coordination as such that is the pivotal consideration but rather the difference in the direction of the dependency at issue.

If the mind were "nothing but" the machinations of matter, if brain psychology were *all* there is to it, then mind would be unable to accomplish its characteristic work of providing a bridge for the domain of physical processes to the domain of ideas. We would never get from here (*physicality*) to there (*thought*): all possibility of achieving meaning, significance, and gaining information would be lost. Whoever insists on seeing the mind as altogether "reduced" to matter thereby excludes the conceptual domain.

8

Pragmatism and Practical Rationality

Functionalistic Pragmatism

Pragmatism is a philosophical position that puts practice at center stage and sees efficacy in practical activities as the prime goals of human endeavor. But there are two markedly different ways of working out this sort of a program.

One way of implementing the leading idea of pragmatism is to see theory and theorizing as being incidental and secondary in importance—a "merely intellectual" concern that has a less significant role in human affairs than do matters of action and praxis. This version of the position might be characterized as *practicalism*.

However, a quite different version of pragmatism sees theory as subordinate to praxis not in *importance* but rather in *fundamentality*. This approach does not relegate theory to a secondary status in point of interest or importance. On the contrary, it regards theory as something crucial and critically important but then takes success in matters of practical implementation as the adequacy criterion of successful theorizing. This criteriological version of the theory might be designated as *functionalism*.

Such a functionalistic version of pragmatism regards effective praxis as the arbiter of appropriate theorizing. It takes considerations of purposive effectiveness to provide the standard for the adequacy of the operative principles of human endeavor—alike in theoretical and practical matters. Effective implementation is its pervasive standard of adequacy. Pragmatism's historic concern has always been not with the descriptive characteristics of things but with their normative appropriateness. And here its logical starting point is the uncontroversial idea that the natural and sensible standard of approval for something that is in any procedural—anything that has an aspect that is methodological, procedural, or instrumental—lies in the question of its successful application. Any process or procedure that has a teleology—that is, an instrumentality for the realization of certain purposes—will automatically be subject to an evaluation standard that looks to its efficacy. For whenever something is in any way purposively oriented to the realization of certain ends, the natural question for its evaluation in this regard is that of its serviceability in effective end realization.

After all, man is a purposive animal. Virtually everything that we do has a purpose to it. Even play, idleness, and tomfoolery have a purpose—to divert, to provide rest and recreation, to kill time.

And certainly our larger projects in the realm of human endeavor are purposive:

Inquiry—to resolve doubt and to guide action.

Ethics—to encourage modes of conduct in human interactions that canalize them into a generally satisfactory and beneficial form.

Law—to establish and enforce rules of conduct.

Education—to acculturate the younger generation so as to enhance the prospect that young people will find their way to personally satisfying and communally beneficial lifestyles.

Art—to create objects or object types, exposure to which engenders personally rewarding and enlightening experiences.

On this basis, a functionalistic pragmatism can encompass the entire range of human concern. It is not (and should not be) a mainly materialistic doctrine concerned only with crass payoffs. Rather, it is a multipurpose resource. For a pragmatic approach to validation can of course be implemented in *any* purposive setting. Given any aim or objective whatever, we can always provide a correlative validation in terms of the effectiveness and efficiency of its realization. But a really thorough pragmatism must dig yet more deeply. It cannot simply take purposes as given—as gift horses into whose mouths we must not look. For purpose adoption too has to be viewed in a pragmatic perspective as an act or activity of sorts that itself stands in need of legitimation. Accordingly, a sensible pragmatism also requires an *axiology of purposes*, a normative methodology for assessing the appropriateness of the purposes we espouse for creatures situated as we are in the world's scheme of things.

We humans live subject to a manifold of processes: physical, chemical, biological, social, economic, and so on. Each processual realm imposes various purposes upon us, subjecting us to needs, requirements, and desiderata of various sorts. The meeting of these purposes involves us in a wide variety of projects, each with its own manifold of purpose-accommodating processes. We are thus committed to such projects as the pursuit of nourishment, of physical security, of comfort, of education, of sociability, of rest and recreation, each designed to meet our requirements for food, shelter, clothing, knowledge, companionship, realization, and equipment with its own complex of needs and desiderata. And throughout this manifold we encounter the same rationale of end realization with its inherent involvement with issues of effectiveness and efficiency. Pragmatism's concern for functional efficiency, for success in the realization of ends and purposes, is an inescapable formative factor as an intelligent being makes its way in the world by means of the instrumentality of rational agency. In such a purposive setting, the pragmatic approach with its concern for functional efficacy is a critical aspect of rationality itself.

The fact of it is that human beings not only have wants, wishes, and desires, they have needs as well. Individually, we need nourishment, physical security, and congenial interaction if our physical and our psychological well-being is to be achieved and maintained. Collectively, we require social arrangements that maximize the opportunities for mutual aid and minimize those for mutual harm. This aspect of the practical scheme of things is built into our very condition as the sorts of creatures we are.

Some aims and purposes are optional—we choose them freely. But others are mandatory—built into the very fabric of our existence within nature as members of our species. These nonoptional aims and purposes will obviously have to play a pivotal role in a functionalistic pragmatism built on that paramount demand of reason: efficacy in goal attainment.

And this endows functionalistic pragmatism with a second dimension of objectivity. On the one hand, it is perfectly objective and nowise a matter of preference what sorts of means are effective in the realization of specified objectives. And on the other hand, it is analogously perfectly objective and nowise a matter of preference that humans have certain needs—certain requirements that must be satisfied if they are to exist, perdure, and function effectively as the sorts of creatures that they have evolved into on the world's stage.

By virtue of their very nature as purposive instrumentalities, the values that reflect our needs can and generally do fall within the domain of reason. For values are functional objects that have a natural teleology themselves, namely that of helping us to lead lives that are personally satisfying (meet our individual needs) and communally productive (facilitate the realizations of constructive goals to the community at large). This state of things has far-reaching implications because it indicates that our assessment of values themselves can and should be ultimately pragmatic. Our evaluations are appropriate only insofar as their adoption and cultivation are efficiently and effectively conducive to the realization of human interests—the rationally appropriate ends, personal and communal—that root us in our place in the scheme of things.

Accordingly, a pragmatism that is consistent, coherent, and self-sustaining will not just proceed pragmatically with respect to achieving unevaluated ends and purposes. It must also apply its pragmatic perspective to the issue of validating ends and purposes themselves in terms of their capacity to facilitate the realization of those considerations, which for us humans are simply "facts of life."

Evaluative Rationality and Appropriate Ends

But how far can this line of thought carry us? Pragmatism's standard of adequacy pivots on procedural efficacy. But can this seemingly crass prioritization of utility possibly provide grounds for even acknowledging the significance in human affairs of higher, less crassly utilitarian sorts of values? Can it ever reach beyond the sphere of the bare basic necessities of life?

To resolve this question we must go back to basics. Pragmatism pivots the validation of our instrumentalities of thought and action on their effectiveness in goal realization. But goals are certainly not created equal; they clearly have different degrees of merit. There are impersonally valid modes of evaluation by which goals themselves can be assessed, so that the rational evaluation that pragmatism envisions can be implemented in an objectively cogent way. The capacity for intelligent choice makes us humans into rational agents, but it is only through our having appropriate values that the prospect of intelligent choice becomes open for us. The human situation being what it is, existential circumstances spread a vast range of possibilities out before us. At many junctures, life confronts us with alternative directions in which to proceed. And only through the evaluation of such alternatives can we affect a sensible (rationally appropriate and acceptable) choice among them. On this basis, values are instrumentalities that serve to possibilize and facilitate the satisfactory conduct of life. And moreover, a commitment to values not only aids in making our lives as intelligent agents possible, they also make it meaningful. For the life of the human individual is brief: here today, gone tomorrow. It is through our commitment to values that we can reach out beyond the restrictive limits of the space and time available to us as individuals in this world, moving toward the realization of something larger and more significant.

To be sure, it is often said that values are just matters of taste—of mere personal predilection. If this were indeed the case, then any and all claims to value objectivity would at once become untenable. But is it so? Evaluation certainly is not—and should not be—a matter of taste. People who are not prepared to back an option of X over Y by *cogent reasons* of some sort are merely evincing a preference and not actually making any sort of meaningful evaluation at all. Tastes, as usually understood, represent unreasoned preferences and purely subjective predilections. There is consequently no disputing about them: *de gustibus non disputandum est.* If I prefer *X* to *Y*, then that's that. But values are something quite different. They are by nature functional instrumentalities since their mission is to canalize our action via our rational choices. They have objective impact, relating not to what we *do prefer* but to what we *can and should appropriately deem preferable*—that is, worthy of preference. And preference worthiness is something that is always discussible, something that needs to be reasoned about. To be in a position to maintain—in a manner that is sensible and reasonable—that *X* is preferable to *Y*, one must be in a position to back one's claim up with some sort of rationale. And the inherent rationality of our need-embedded evaluations carries them outside the range of mere matters of taste.

Moreover, our values themselves are not—and should not be—arbitrary and haphazard. For in the final analysis, they pivot not on mere wants and the vagaries of arbitrary choice in fortuitous preference but on our best interests and real needs—on what is necessary or advantageous to a person's well-being. We humans, being the sorts of creatures we are, have need-based interests that as such should (insofar as we are rational) control the validation of our wants and preferences. Validating an evaluation thus is not and cannot be a matter of mere subjectivity. The projects into which our nature impels us—the medical project, say, or the alimentary, or the cognitive—obviously carry a whole host of value commitments in their wake. Just here is where the pragmatic impetus comes into play. For once a goal is given, then other connected goals can come to be validated with reference to it. It is thus a grave mistake to think that one cannot reason about values on the supposed ground that values are simply a matter of taste and thus beyond the reach of reason because "there's no reasoning about tastes." Such a position founders on the distinction between mere wants and real needs. For the fact is that values are valid just exactly to the extent they serve to implement and satisfy our needs and our correlatively appropriate interests. (The seeming harshness of this view is mitigated by the circumstance that for us humans the satisfaction of some of our mere wants—seen not in specific but in statistical generality—is itself a need.)

In particular, values that impede the realization of a person's best interests are clearly inappropriate. A priority scheme that sets mere wants above real needs or sets important objectives aside to avert trivial inconveniences is thereby deeply flawed from the rational point of view.[1] And even as with needs and interests in general, so even great values may well have to yield to the yet greater. (Some things are rightly dearer to sensible people than life itself.)

And, to reemphasize, the rationality of ends inheres in the simple fact that we humans have various valid *needs*—that we require not only nourishment and protection against the elements for the maintenance of health, but also information ("cognitive orientation"), affection, freedom of action, and much else besides. Without such varied goods we cannot thrive as fulfilled human beings. The person who does not give these manifold desiderata their due—who may even set out to frustrate their realization—is clearly not being rational. For in the end, evaluation lies at the very heart and core of rationality. For rationality is a matter of best serving our overall interests. The person who expends more effort in the pursuit of ends than they are worth is not just being wasteful but foolish, which is to say irrational. The rationality of our actions hinges critically on both the appropriateness of our ends *and* the suitability of the means by which we pursue their cultivation. Both of these components—the *cogently cognitive* ("*intelligent* pursuit") and the *normatively purposive* ("*appropriate* ends")—are alike essential to full-fledged rationality.

To be sure, the springs of human agency are diverse. We frequently act not for *reasons* alone but from "mere motives"—out of anxiety, cupidity, habit, impulse. In such cases, we also have ends and purposes in view—but generally not *appropriate* ones. If rationality were merely a matter of unevaluated goals and purposes as such—if it were to consist simply in the "technical rationality" of goal-efficient action—then the established line between the rational and the irrational would have to be redrawn in a very different place, and its linkage with what is intelligent and well-advised would be severed. But where there is no *appropriate* and thus no meaningful end, rational agency ceases. (There may, of course, still be room for goal-directed action, but without goals it is bound to be problematic from the rational point of view.) And of course while all people are (hopefully) *capable* of reason, no well-informed person thinks they invariably—or even generally—exercise this capacity.

But the fact remains that the rationality of ends is an indispensable component of rationality at large for two principal reasons. Rationally valued ends must be evaluatively appropriate ones: if we adopt inappropriate ends we are not being rational, no matter how efficiently and effectively we pursue them. The sensible attunement of means to ends that is characteristic of rationality calls for an appropriate balancing of costs and benefits in our choice among alternative ways of resolving our cognitive, practical, and evaluative problems. Reason accordingly demands determination of the true value of things. Even as cognitive reason requires that in determining what we are to accept we should assess the evidential grounds for theses at their true worth, so evaluative reason requires us to appraise the values of our practical options at their true worth in determining what we are to choose or prefer. And this calls for an appropriate cost-benefit analysis. Values must be managed as an overall "economy" in a rational way to achieve overall harmonization and optimization. Economic rationality is not the only sort of rationality there is, but it is an important aspect of overall rationality. Someone who rejects such economic considerations—who, in the absence of any envisioned compensating advantages, deliberately purchases benefits for millions he recognizes as being worth only a few pennies—is simply not rational. It is just as irrational to let one's efforts in the pursuit of chosen objectives incur costs that outrun their true worth as it is to let one's beliefs run afoul of the evidence. And the evaluative rationality at issue here is the pragmatic one of the efficient pursuit of appropriate ends.[2]

After all, there is nothing automatically appropriate—let alone sacred—about our own ends, objectives, and preferences as such. We can be every bit as irrational and stupid with the adoption of ends as with any other choice. Apparent interests are not automatically real, getting what one wants is not necessarily to one's benefit, and goals are not rendered valid by their mere adoption. People's ends can be self-destructive, self-defeating impediments to the realization of their true needs. For rationality, the crucial question is that of the true value of the item at issue. What counts for rational validity is not preference but preferability—not what people do want, but what they *ought* to want; not what *people* actually want, but what *sensible* or *right-thinking* people would want under the circumstances. The normative aspect is ineliminable here. Rationality calls for objective judgment—for an assessment of preferability, rather than for a mere expression of preference, no questions asked. The rationality of ends, their rational appropriateness and legitimacy, is accordingly a crucial aspect of rationality. More is at issue with rationality than a matter of strict instrumentality—mere effectiveness in the pursuit of ends no matter how inappropriate they may be. When we impute to our ends a weight and value they do not in fact have, we pursue mere will-o'-the-wisps. There is an indissoluble connection between the true value of something (its being good or right or useful) and its being rational to choose or prefer this thing. Being desired does not automatically make something desirable, nor being valued valuable. The pivot is how matters *ought* to be—a region where needs come to dominate over wants.

And so, the crucial question for evaluative rationality is not that of what we prefer, but that of what is in our best interests—not simply what we may happen to desire, but what is good for us in the sense of fostering the realization of our needs. The pursuit of what we want is rational only in so far as we have *sound* reasons for deeming this to be deserving of want. The question whether what we prefer is preferable, in the sense of *deserving* this preference, is always relevant. For it is not just beliefs that can be stupid, ill-advised, and inappropriate—that is to say, *irrational*—but ends as well.

The Impetus of Interests

Contentions like "Smith is selfish, inconsiderate, and boorish" accordingly do not lie outside the sphere of rational inquiry—nor for that matter do contentions like "Behavior that is selfish/inconsiderate/boorish is against the best interest of people." The issue of *appropriate* action in the circumstances in which we find ourselves is pivotal for rationality. Be it in matters of belief, action, or evaluation, we want—that is to say, often do and always *should* want—to do the best we can. One cannot be rational without due care for the desirability of what one desires—the issue of its alignment with our *real*, as distinguished from our *putative*, or merely seeming interests.

But just what is it that is in a person's real or best interests? Partly, this is indeed a matter of meeting the needs that people universally have in common—health, satisfactory functioning of body and mind, adequate resources, human companionship and affection, and so on.[3] Partly, it is a matter of the particular role one plays: cooperative children are in the interests of a parent, customer loyalty in those of a shopkeeper. Partly, it is a matter of what one simply happens to want. (If John loves Mary, then engaging Mary's attention and affections are in John's interests—some sorts of things are in a person's interests simply because he takes an interest in them.) But these want-related interests are valid only by virtue of their relation to universal interests. Mary's approbation is in John's interest only because having the approbation of someone we love is *always* in *anyone's* interest. Any valid *specific* interest must fall within the validating scope of an appropriate *universal* covering principle of interest legitimation. (The development of my stamp collection is in my interest only because it is part of a hobby that constitutes an avocation for me and securing adequate relaxation and diversion from the stresses and annoyances of one's daily cares is something that is in *anyone's* interests.)

But what of those "mere whims and fancies"? If I have a craving for eating crabgrass, then is my doing so not a perfectly appropriate "interest" of mine? Yes, it is. But only because it is covered by perfectly cogent universal interest, namely that of "Doing what I feel like doing in circumstances where neither injury to me nor harm to others is involved." A specific (concrete, particular) interest of a person is valid as such only if it can be subordinated to a universal interest by way of having a basis in people's legitimate needs. It is these higher-level principles that are the controlling factors from the standpoint of reason. Only through coming under the aegis of those larger universal needs can our idiosyncratic want come to be validated.

Like various beliefs, various evaluations are palpably crazy.[4] Reason, after all, is not just a matter of the compatibility or consistency of pre-given commitments but of the warrant that there is for undertaking certain commitments in the first place. An *evaluative* rationality that informs us that certain preferences are absurd—preferences that wantonly violate our nature, impair our being, or diminish our opportunities—fortunately lies within the human repertoire.

The ancient Greek thinker, Xenophanes of Colophon, was doubtless right. Even as different creatures may well have different gods, so they might well have different goods. But no matter. *For us humans* the perfectly appropriate sort of good is *our* sort of good—the human good inherent in the manner of our emplacement within the world's scheme of things. In this regard, Aristotle did indeed get to the heart of the matter. For us, the human good is indeed an adequate foundation for substantive, practical rationality. Given that we are what we are, it is this that is decisive for us. We have to go on from where we are. It is in *this* sense alone that there is no deliberation about ends. The universally appropriate ends at issue in our human condition are not somehow freely *chosen* by us; they are fixed by the inescapable (for us) ontological circumstance that—like it or not—we find ourselves to exist as human beings, and thus able to function as free rational agents. Their ultimate inherence in (generic) human needs determines the appropriateness of our particular, individual ends and thereby endows a functionalistic pragmatism with a broadly humanistic value orientation.

We humans are so situated that from *our* vantage point (and who else's can be decisive for us?) various factors can and should be seen as goods—as aspects or components of what is in itself a quintessentially good end in its relation to us. Without achieving such goods, we cannot thrive as human beings—we cannot achieve the condition of well-being that Aristotle called "flourishing." Flourishing as *humans*, as the sorts of creatures we are, patently is *for us* an intrinsic good (though not, to be sure, necessarily the supreme good). It "comes with the territory" so to speak, being mandated for us by our place in nature's scheme of things. And this desideratum is itself multifaceted in serving as an umbrella goal that can carry others in its wake. It must, after all, come to be particularized to the concrete situation of specific individuals and thereby becomes complex and variegated.

To be sure, a person's "appropriate interests" will have a substantial sector of personal relativity. One person's self-ideal, shaped in the light of his own value structure, will—quite appropriately—be different from that of another. And, moreover, what sorts of interests someone has will hinge in significant measure on the particular circumstances and conditions in which they find themselves—including their wishes and desires. (In the *absence* of any countervailing considerations, getting what I want is in my best interests.) All the same, there is also a large body of real interests that people not only share in common but must pursue in common—for example, as regards standard of living (health and resources) and quality of life (opportunities and conditions). And both sorts of interests—the idiosyncratic and the generic—play a determinative role in the operations of rationality. And both must accordingly figure in a sensible pragmatism's concern for the efficacious realization of our valid objectives.[5]

9

The Demands of Morality

The Functional/Purposive Nature of Morality

The pervasive relativism of the age views moral principles and standards as little more than a matter of custom based on practical convenience, like the rules of the road for driving—useful devices to diminish conflict in contexts of human interaction, but lacking any deeper validation and legitimacy, and certainly without any claims to universality. Morality as regarded from this angle is predicated on local custom, as part of the mores of the group. And any such behavioral code is as good as any other: it is simply a matter of "When in Rome do as the Romans do." All moralities are created equal. There is no place for moral objectivity.

And so, nowadays a widespread but nevertheless unfortunate tendency to deny the possibility of rational controversy about moral matters prevails, relegating morality to the never-never land of matters of taste, feeling, or otherwise discursively insupportable opinion. Such a view is profoundly inappropriate. But once one recognizes the *functional* aspect of morality—as inculcating actions that safeguard the real interest of people—then moral issues become open to rational deliberation.[1] This functional aspect of morality, its very nature representing an inherently appropriate, end-oriented project, blocks the prospect of indifferentism or of a relativistically detached view of morality as a mere matter of individual inclination or of "the customs of the tribe."

But such a radically subjective view along the lines that "With moral issues there is only what people think; there just are no objective facts of the matter" is ultimately untenable for anyone who, rejecting nihilism, gives credence to some sort of morality or other. For one cannot consistently look on one's own moral convictions as "merely matters of opinion." In doing this one would thereby ipso facto fail to accept them as such—that is, as *moral* convictions. In view of what can possibly qualify as such, it lies in the very nature of our moral judgments that we regard them as justified via a rationale regarding what is required by due heed of the interests of people.

Morality, after all, is an end-governed purposive enterprise—one that is structured by its having a characteristic functional mission of transparent appropriateness. For it is morality's object to equip people with a body of norms (rules and values) that make for peaceful and collectively satisfying coexistence by facilitating their living together and interacting in a way that is productive for the realization of the "general benefit"—of the wider community as a whole. The pursuit of righteousness that constitutes morality is like the pursuit of health that constitutes medicine—both are projects with an inherent teleology of their own, geared to fostering patterns of action and interaction that promote the best interests of people in general.

The functional nature of morality means that being *thought* to be morally appropriate no more makes a certain action to be so than being *thought* to be medically effective or transportationally efficient would render a certain practice to be so. The claim that a rule or practice is morally appropriate—that in the conditions prevailing in a society it is effective in serving and enhancing the real interests of people in general—is thoroughly objective and "factual." One is thus rationally constrained by considerations of mere self-consistency to see one's own moral position as rationally superior to the available alternatives. If one did not take this stance—did not deem one's moral position to be effectively optimal—then one could not see oneself as rationally justified in adopting it, so that it would, in consequence, fail to be one's own real moral position, contrary to hypothesis.[2] Because the claims of morality are categorical, to see morality as subjective is in fact to abandon it.

The validity of most moral appraisals is accordingly something that is objectively determinable and nowise lies in the eye of the beholder. For someone to say, "You acted wrongly in stealing that money" is *not* simply for them to assert that you stole the money and additionally to evince disapprobation and urge a different sort of future conduct, but rather—and most importantly—to *indicate a reason* for acting differently. For the claim implies that your act instantiates a type of behavior (namely, stealing) that does injury to the legitimate interests of others. And this issue of human needs and benefits, of people's real *interests*, such as their physical and psychological well being, is not a matter of subjective reaction. What is in our interest—what is *advantageous* for our long-term, overall physical and psychological well-being, given the sorts of creatures we are—is in large measure a factual issue capable of empirical inquiry that lies open to general, public investigation.

Morality is by its very nature geared to safeguarding the interests of others as best we can manage it in prevailing circumstances. And people do not *choose* what it is that is in their interests.[3]

After all, physicians, parents, public officials, and others constantly concern themselves with issues of what is good for people—what enables them to thrive and lead satisfying lives. People themselves are by no means themselves the definitive authorities regarding what is in their interests—their doctor, lawyer, or financial advisor can know a good deal more about these interests than the individuals themselves. In the final analysis, the objectivity of *moral* evaluations thus resides in the very nature of the issue. People are no doubt the definitive authorities regarding what *pleases* them, but certainly not regarding what *benefits* them. And this objectivity of people's interests carries in its wake also the objectivity of interest promotion—and thus of morality. We thus cannot detach rational justification from objective validity in the moral sphere, because to say that a person is (rationally) justified in making a judgment is to say that he or she is (rationally) entitled to take it to be objectively true or correct. Nor can we detach objective validity from factuality, for where there is no appropriate claim to objective factuality (no "fact of the matter"), there can be no justification or endorsement either—though, to be sure, the facts of the matter may happen to be *evaluative* facts.

What renders morality objective is thus the fact that moral evaluations can—and should—be validated as cogent through considerations of purposive efficacy. To claim that someone ought (or ought not) to act in a certain way is thereby to commit oneself to the availability of a *good reason* why one should or should not do so, and a reason that is not only good but good in a certain mode, the moral mode, shows that this sort of action is bound up with due care for the interest of others. And this matter of interest is something open to general view—something that can be investigated by other people as readily as by the agent. For since people's (real) interests are rooted in their needs, the morally crucial circumstance that certain modes of action are conducive and others deleterious to the best interests of people is something that can be investigated, evidentiated, and sensibly assessed by the standards generally prevalent in rational discussion and controversy. The matters are not questions of feeling or taste but represent something objective about which one can deliberate and argue in a sensible way on the basis of reasons whose cogency are, or should be, accessible to anyone. The modes of behavior of people that render life in their communities "nasty, brutish, and short" (or indeed even merely more difficult and less pleasant than need be) generally admit of straightforward and unproblematic discernment.

Uniformity Despite Diversity

And yet there are some complications here. For moral *pluralism* is unavoidable, and moral codes can appropriately differ from one society to another. Do these facts not entail an indifferentist relativism to the effect that, in principle, "anything goes," by making morality into what is ultimately just a matter of local custom?

By no means! All modes of morality have important elements in common simply in view of the fact that *morality* is at issue. Since (by hypothesis) they all qualify as "modes of morality," they are bound to encompass such fundamental considerations as the following:

- What people do matters. Some actions are right, others wrong, some acceptable and some not. There is an important difference here.

- This is not just a product of convention, custom, and the thing to do. Violations of moral principles are not just offenses against sensibility but against people's just claims in matters where people's actual well-being is at stake.

- In violating the moral rules, we inflict injury on the life, welfare, or otherwise legitimate interests of others—either actually or by way of putting them unjustifiably at risk.

Attunement to considerations of this sort is *by definition* essential to any system of "morality," and it serves to provide the basis for imperatives like: "Do not simply ignore other people's rights and claims in your own deliberations," "Do not inflict needless pain on people," "Honor the legitimate interests of others," "Do not take what rightfully belongs to others without their appropriately secured consent," "Do not wantonly break promises," "Do not cause someone anguish simply for your own amusement." In the context of *morality*, principles and rules of this sort are universal and absolute. They are of the very essence of morality; in abandoning them we would withdraw from a discussion of *morality* and would, in effect, be changing the subject. What we say might be interesting—and even true—but it would deal with another topic.

"But moral objectivity is surely counterindicated by the circumstance that one cannot validly criticize the moral code of a society by any 'external' criteria." By no means! Whether a certain operational code is intended within the ambit of its social context to operate as a moral code may well be a proper subject of discussion and controversy. But once it is settled that it is indeed a *moral* code that is at issue, then in view of that very fact one can certainly bring principles of critical evaluation to bear. For at this point the question becomes paramount whether—and how effectively—this code accomplishes for its society those functions for which moral codes are instituted among men—to constrain their interactions into lines that safeguard their best interests.

When we are assessing a moral code in this way, we are *not* simply exercising a cultural imperialism by judging it against our own in asking how concordant or discordant it is with the prevailing moral standards of our environing group. We are judging it, rather, against those universal and "absolute" standards in terms of which the adequacy of any code, our own included, must be appraised. The evaluation of appropriateness is not one of ours against theirs, but one of judging *both* ours and theirs by a common, generic standard. What makes an action right or wrong (as the case may be) is just exactly the issue of whether doing the sort of thing at issue injures or protects the interests of all the agents concerned. (To reemphasize: morality is by definition geared to the benefit of rational agents, even as refrigeration is by definition geared to cooling.[4]) This is part and parcel of the very meaning of "morally right" and "morally wrong." And it renders judgment in these matters factual, objective, and rationally disputable.

Morality, to reemphasize, is a particular, well-defined sort of purposive project, whose cohesive unity as such resides in its inherent function of molding the behavior of people in line with a care for one another's interests. Even as there are many ways to build houses, fuel automobiles, and so on, so there are various ways of being moral. But that surely does not mean that there is no overarching unity of goals, functions, principles, and values to lend a definitional cohesion to the enterprise. Moral behavior can take many forms, but morality itself is a uniform project! But in fact, moral variability is more apparent than real—an absolute uniformity does, and must, prevail at the level of fundamentals. "Act with due heed of the interests of others" is a universal and absolute moral principle whose working out in different contexts will, to be sure, very much depend on just exactly how the interests of people happen to be reciprocally intertwined. But despite the diversity of the substantive moral codes of different societies, the basic overarching principles of morality are uniform and invariant—inherent in the very idea of what morality is all about.

Accordingly, different "moralities" are simply diverse implementations of certain uniform, overarching moral *principles*. There is ample room for situational variation and pluralism in response to the question: "What is the morally appropriate thing to do?" But there is no such room with respect to: "What is morality—and what principles are at issue here?" The concept of morality and its contents are fixed by the *questioner's prerogative* inherent in the principle that it is the inquirer's own conception of the matter that determines what is at issue. In *our deliberations* about moral rights and wrongs it is thus *our conception* of "morality" and its governing principles that is conclusive for what is at issue. When *we* engage in deliberations about morality—be it our own or that of others—it is "morality" *as we understand it* that figures in this discussion.[5] And this circumstance of theoretic fixity engenders the stability of those project-definitive moral principles.

The Hierarchical Dimension

But how could one plausibly pivot the issue of moral objectivity on the very idea of what "morality" is all about? After all, different people have different ideas about this. Of course, different people do think differently about morality, even as they think differently about dogs or automobiles. But that's basically irrelevant. What is at issue with "morality" as such does not lie with you or with me but with all of us. What matters here is how the word is actually used in the community—in the language in which our discussion of the issue transpires. What matters is not what people think about the topic, but how they use the terminology that defines it.

Yet how can this fixity of the conception of morality and of the basic principles that are at issue within it—inherent in the monolithic uniformity of "what *morality* is"—be reconciled with the plain fact of a pluralistic diversity of (presumably cogent) answers to the question: "What is it moral to do?" How can such an absolutism of morality's fundamentals coexist with the patent relativity of moral evaluations across different times and cultures?

At this point we have to return to the idea of a "cultivation hierarchy." For in the case of normality too, we have to deal with a descending hierarchy of characterizing aims, fundamental principles and values, governing rules, implementing directives, and (finally) particular rulings (see display 9.1). And the answer to our question

Display 9.1. The Stratification Levels of the Implementation Hierarchy for Moral Norms

LEVEL 1	CHARACTERIZING AIMS	"due care for the best interests of others"
LEVEL 2	GOVERNING PRINCIPLES AND VALUES	"honesty," "candor"
LEVEL 3	GOVERNING RULES	"Do not lie," "Speak truthfully"
LEVEL 4	OPERATING DIRECTIVES (GROUNDRULES OF PROCEDURE)	"When declaring what you believe do not do so misleadingly"
LEVEL 5	PARTICULAR RULINGS	"Answer Jones truthfully (as best you can)"

lies in the fact that several intermediate levels or strata inevitably separate those overarching "basic principles of morality" from any concrete judgments about what it is moral to do.

At the topmost level we have the defining aims of morality, the objectives that identify the moral enterprise as such by determining its nature and specifying the aims and objectives that characterize what morality is all about (for example: "Act with a view to safeguarding the valid interests of others."). These characterizing aims of morality represent the overarching "defining objectives" of the entire enterprise that characterize the project as such. They explicate what is at issue when it is *morality* (rather than basket weaving) that we propose to concern ourselves with. In spelling out the fundamental idea of what morality is all about, these top-level norms provide the ultimate reference points of moral deliberation. And they are unalterably fixed—inherent in the very nature of the subject.

And these fundamental "aims of the enterprise" also fix the basic principles and controlling values that delineate the moral virtues (honesty, trustworthiness, civility, probity, and the rest). Such values define the salient norms that link the abstract characterizing aims to an operational morality of specific governing rules. The norms embodied in these basic principles and values are "universal" and "absolute," serving as parts of what makes morality the thing it is (examples include: "Do not violate the duly established rights and claims of others." "Do not unjustly deprive others of life, liberty, or opportunity for self-development." "Do not tell self-serving falsehoods." "Do not deliberately aid and abet others in wrongdoing."). Accordingly, these high-level principles also lie fixedly in the very nature of the subject. At these two topmost levels, then, there is simply no room for any "disagreement about morality." Here disagreement betokens misunderstanding: if one does not recognize the fundamental aims, principles, and values that characterize the moral enterprise as such, then one is simply talking about something else altogether. In any discussion of *morality* these things are simply *givens*. But this situation changes as one moves further down the list and takes additional steps in the descent to concreteness.

At the next (third) level, we encounter the governing rules and regulations that direct the specifically moral transaction of affairs. Here, we have the generalities of the usual and accustomed sort: "Do not lie," "Do not cheat," "Do not steal," and so on. At this level we come to the imperatives that guide our deliberations and decisions. Like the Ten Commandments, they set out the controlling dos and don'ts of the moral practice of a community, providing us with general guidance in moral conduct. Here, variability begins to set in. For these rules implement morality's ruling principles at the concrete level of recommended practices in a way that admits of adjustment to the fluid circumstances of local conditions. A generalized moral rule on the order of the injunction "Do not steal" (or "Do not take something that properly belongs to another") is in itself still something abstract and schematic. It still requires the concrete fleshing out of substantive implementing specifications to tell us what sorts of things make for "proper ownership." And so the next (fourth) level presents us with the ground rules of procedure or implementing directives that furnish our working guidelines and criteria for the moral resolution of various types of cases (for example: "Killing is wrong except in cases of self-defense or under legal mandate as in war or execution."). At this level of implementing standards and criteria, the variability of local practice comes to the fore, so that there is further room for pluralistic diversification here; we ourselves implement "Do not lie, avoid telling falsehoods," by way of "Say what you believe (to be the case)," but a society of convinced sceptics could not do so. The operating ground rules of level four thus incorporate the relative, situational standards and criteria though which the more abstract, higher-level rules get their grip on concrete situations. Those general rules themselves are too abstract—too loose or general to be applicable without further directions to give them a purchase on concrete situations. They must be given concrete implementation with reference to local—and thus variable—arrangements.[6]

Finally, at the lowest (fifth) level, we come to the particular moral rulings, the individual resolutions with respect to the specific issues arising in concrete cases (for example: "It was wicked of Lady Macbeth to incite her husband to kill the king.").

In such an "implementation hierarchy," we thus descend from what is abstractly and fixedly universal to what is concrete and variable. Level two is contained in level one simply by way of exfoliative "explication." But as we move downward, past level three to the implementing specifications of level four, there is—increasingly—a looseness or "slack" that makes room for the specific and variable ways of different groups for implementing the particular higher-level objective at issue.

The entire hierarchy contention culminates in a single, overreaching ruling imperative ("Support the interests of people!") that stands correlative with an enterprise-determinative value ("the best interests of people"). This overarching concern does not itself stand subordinate to further moral rules. After all, it is only possible up to a certain point that we can have rules for applying rules and principles for applying principles. The process of validating lower-level considerations in terms of higher-level ones must come to a stop somewhere. And with such implementation hierarchies, it is the overarching controlling teleology of "the aim of the entire enterprise" that gives at once unity and determinatives to the justificatory venture.

Note the element of abstract generality imposes the need for some suitable qualification above the bottom level of concrete particularity. Here some sort of qualification like "needless" or "unnecessary" or "inappropriate" (in their contraries) will be operative. The sorts of things that keep harms and so forth from being needless are clear enough. They include qualifications like "merely for personal convenience," "for one's own gain," "for one's own pleasure," "out of perversity or ill will," and so on. To be sure, the list of inadequate reasons that render harms morally inappropriate is potentially endless, but the sort of thing at issue is clear enough to anyone but a moral imbecile.

Overall then, we have to deal with a chain of subordination linkages that connect a concrete moral judgment—a particular moral act recommendation or command—with the ultimate defining aim of the moral enterprise. The long and short of it is that any appropriate moral injunction must derive its validity through being an appropriate instantiation or concretization of an overarching principle of universal (unrestricted) validity under which it is subsumed. It must, in short, represent a circumstantially appropriate implementation of the fixities of absolute morality. Thus, even as in Roman Catholic theology there is a "hierarchy of truths" that places different teachings of the Church at different levels of doctoral essentiality or fundamentality, so in the present context there is a comparable hierarchy of imperatival strata that place different injunctions at different levels of fundamentality in the moral enterprise, with some (the basic principles) as, in this setting, absolute and others as variable and relative to context and circumstance. Fundamentals are fixed as essential to the moral domain as such, but agreement on concrete issues is itself something more marginal.

The crucial fact is that one moral value—fairness, for example—can come into operation very differently in different contexts. In an economy of abundance it may militate for equality of shares and in an economy of scarcity for equality of opportunity. The particular circumstances that characterize a context of operation may importantly condition the way in which a moral value or principle can (appropriately) be applied. We cannot expect to encounter any universal consensus across cultural and temporal divides: physicians of different eras are (like moralists) bound to differ—and to some extent those of different cultures as well. There is—inevitably—substantial variability among particular groups, each with its own varying ideas conditioned by locally prevailing conditions and circumstances. But the impact of low-level variation is mitigated by the fact that justification at lower levels proceeds throughout with reference to superordinated standards in a way that makes for higher-level uniformity. Uniform high-level principles will have to be implemented differently in different circumstances. Medicine and morality alike are complex projects unified and integrated amid the welter of changing conditions and circumstances by the determinative predominance of high-level principles.

At the level of basic principles, then, morality is absolute; its strictures at this level hold good for everyone, for all rational agents. And lower-level rules and rulings must—if valid—preserve a "linkage of subsumption" to those highest-level abstractions, a linkage mediated by way of more restrictive modes of implementation. These implementing rules involve contextual relativity—coordination with contingently variable (setting-dependent and era- and culture-variable) circumstances and situations. Thus while moral objectives and basic principles—those top levels of the hierarchy of moral norms—are absolute and universal, "slack" arises as we move further down the ladder, leaving room for (quite appropriate) contextual variability and differentiation. "Do not unjustifiably take the property of another for your own use" is an unquestionably valid principle of absolute morality. But it avails nothing until such time as there are means for determining what is "the property of another" and what constitutes "unjustified taking." "Don't break promises merely for your own convenience" is a universal moral rule and as such is global and absolute. But what sorts of practices constitute making a valid promise is something that is largely determined through localized social conventions and personal principles. Local context—variable history, tradition, expectation-defining legal systems, evaluative commitments, and the like—thus allows for substantial variability at the level of operational rules and codes, of moral practices.

And so, the increasing looseness of fit or "slack" that we encounter as we move toward the bottom level of concreteness makes for considerable context-specific variability. Here, underdetermination may come into play through the existence of plausible reasons for divergent positions without any prospect of categorical resolution one way or the other. A situation of moral indeterminacy may arise where each one of several equally cogent positions can come into irreconcilable conflict. The same respect for life that leads one person to take up arms against a tyrant may lead another to walk in the path of pacifism and self-sacrifice. Either position is defensible, and both deserve moral recognition and respect: in a dispute between these two variant appraisals there is no single unique right answer. In settings of scarcity (battlefield triage situations, for example), there may well be very real morally laden choices—the relief of suffering versus the promotion of survival, for instance—where there is no definitive right or wrong.[7]

Morality's characteristic universality is thus inevitably mediated through factors that are variable, conventional, and culturally relative. That project-definitive general principle must be implemented in concrete circumstances and be adapted to them, even as the idea of hospitality towards strangers, for example, has to function differently in European and in Bedouin culture, seeing that deserts and cities are very different human environments. Still, the deeper moral principles that underlie the moral rules and practices of a society ("Even strangers have their due—they too are entitled to respect, to courtesy, and to assistance in need") transcend the customs of any particular community. As concerns morality, culture is indeed a localizing and differentiating agent—but one that merely conditions those fundamental invariants that are inherent in the very conception of morality as such.

Against Moral Relativism (Anthropological and Others)

Moral relativism proclaims: "We have *our* moral convictions (rules, standards, values) and they have *theirs*. One is every bit as good as the other. To each his own. Nobody is in a position to criticize or condemn the moral views of others."[8] But to take this line at every point as regards moral matters is simply to abandon the very idea of morality. Such a position does indeed hold true with respect to *mores*—we eat with cutlery, they with chopsticks; we sleep on beds, they in hammocks; we speak one language, they another—each with equal propriety. But this indifference does *not* hold for matters of moral principle. "We treat strangers with respect; they (those cannibals) eat them. We treat the handicapped kindly; they drown them at sea. We treat darker-skinned humans as equals; they as inferiors. And the one way of proceeding is just as appropriate as the other. It's all just a matter of local custom." Rubbish! It simply is not true from the moral standpoint! If crass selfishness, pointless maltreatment, wanton deceit, or the infliction of needless pain is wrong for us, it is wrong for them too—and conversely. At the level of fundamentals, matters of moral principle are the same for everyone. What holds good for us holds good for them too. A code that sees every mode of behavior as indifferent—every sort of action as equally acceptable—is by its very nature not a moral code (whatever else it may be).

But what of those cases in which doing the moral thing exacts a price in terms of selfish personal advantage?

One must look on this issue as being much like any other conflict of interest situation. I simply have to decide where my priorities ought to lie, whether with morality or with selfish advantage. And this decision has larger implications for us. For it is not *just* a matter of deciding what I want to do in this case. Because of the divisive nature of the case, it is a matter of deciding *what sort of person I am to be.* For in acting immorally I produce two sorts of results:

- The *direct* result of my action—presumably certain gains that it would secure for me;

- The *indirect* result of making me a person of a certain sort, that is, someone who would do *that* sort of thing to realize that sort of result.

In so acting, I make myself into a person of a certain sort. Even if no one else knows it, the fact still remains that that's what I've done—I've made myself into a person who would do that sort of thing in order to realize that sort of benefit. And my self-respect is (or *ought* to be) of such great value to me that the advantages I could secure by immoral action do not countervail against the losses of self-respect that would be involved.

In acting in a way that I recognize to be wrong, I sustain a loss and (if my head is screwed on straight) sustain it where it counts the most—in my own sight. A vicarious concern for others enriches one's life and makes one not only a better but also a more fully developed person.

Doing what one wants is not automatically a matter of selfishness; that very much depends on what it is that one happens to want. As one recent author points out "while it does sound distinctly odd to say that a person embarked on a life of self-sacrifice and devotion to others is pursuing his own good," there is nothing odd about saying that such a person is leading a life where (as he sees the matter) it is good for him to lead.[9] One's vision of the good can (and should) include arrangements where oneself is not cast in the role of a prime beneficiary.

Surely, there is nothing in any way inherently unreasonable or irrational about a selfless concern for others. Indeed, there is no adequate reason for calling a man unreasonable if his actions militate against his own narrowly selfish advantage. To be sure, a man will be unreasonable, indeed irrational, if his actions systematically impede his objectives. But—convenient oversimplification apart—there is no justification whatever for holding that his *only* rationally legitimate objectives are of the selfish or self-interested sort. It is a travesty for this concept to construe *rationality* in terms of prudential self-advantage. Neither for individuals nor for societies is "the pursuit of happiness" (construed as narrowly selfish pleasure) an appropriate guide to action; its dictates must be counterbalanced by recognizing the importance of doing those things that, in after years, we can look back with justifiable pride.

Just as it is rational to do the *prudent* thing (such as enduring the dentist's ministrations) even if doing so goes against one's immediate selfish desires, so the same holds with doing the *moral* thing. Being a moral person is prominent among our (real) interests. And so, confronted with the choice between the moral and the narrowly selfish, our interests *automatically* lie on the side of the moral choice. Morality is indeed a matter of self-interest, but only if one is prepared to distinguish true (real) from merely apparent interests ("what's good for me" from "what one wants").

But then what of the question: "Why be moral—why do what morality demands?" Here there is in fact a grave ambiguity because the question, "Why be moral?" can be construed in three importantly different ways:

1. from the moral point of view;
2. from the standpoint of *enlightened* prudence, of an intelligent heed of our real interests;
3. from the standpoint of the selfishness of satisfying our desires.

Here as elsewhere, the answer we arrive at depends on which interpretation of the question we use. If we use (1), the answer is simply that morality itself demands it. And if we use (2), the answer is that enlightened prudence also demands it, that our real and truly "best" interests require it for the reasons indicated above. But if we use (3), the situation is quite different. There is no earthly way to validate morality from the standpoint of selfishness, of self-interest *narrowly* construed, in terms of the satisfaction of mere (raw and unevaluated) desires. And this is to be welcomed, not lamented—at any rate from the moral point of view—for the very reason that the being of morality lies in countervailing the siren call of immediate gratification.

All considered, it is point (2) that is crucial here. And in its light the basic question of the relation of morality and rationality may be resolved via the argument:

1. The intelligent cultivation of one's *real* self-interest is quintessentially rational.

2. It is to one's real self-interest to act morally—even if doing so goes against one's immediate selfish desires.

Therefore: It is rational to be moral

There is nothing all that complex about the relationship of rationality and morality. We have, more or less by definition:

Rationality: doing the *intelligent* thing (in matters of belief, action, and evaluation).

Morality: doing the *right* thing (in regard to action affecting the interest of others).

The concordance of morality with rationality is established through the fact that the intelligent thing to do and the right thing to do will ultimately coincide.

To forego rationality is to abandon (as best we can tell) the intelligent cultivation of appropriate interests. Given the fact that we have a genuine interest in being the sort of person who cares for the interests of others, morality is part of the package. The rational person will also be morally good—conscientious, compassionate, kind—because their own best interest is served thereby, seeing that they have a real and sizable stake in being the sort of person who can take rational satisfaction in the contemplation of their own way of life.

"But what if I just don't happen to be the sort of person who gets satisfaction from contemplating the quality of my life and its constituent actions?" Then not only can we feel sorry for you, but we are (normatively) justified in setting your stake in the matter as naught. Your stance is like that of someone who says: "Appropriate human values mean nothing to me." Your position seems afraid of that most basic of rational imperatives: to realize oneself as the sort of creature one happens to be. In being profoundly unintelligent, such a stance is profoundly irrational as well.

In the final analysis then, to act immorally is to act unreasonably because it compromises one's true interests—partly for Hobbesian reasons (fouling one's own nest) and partly for Platonic ones (failing to realize one's human potential).

Such a position is substantially identical with that which Plato attributed of Socrates in the *Republic*: that being unjust and immoral—regardless of what immediate benefits it may gain for us—is always ultimately disadvantageous because of the damage it does to our character (or *psyche*) by making us into the sort of person we ourselves cannot really respect. ("What profiteth a man if he should gain the whole world, but lose his own soul?") On such a view it is not the case that the impetus of morality subsists through its *rewards*: either intrinsic ("virtue is its own reward") or prudential. We should be moral not because it (somehow) pays, but because we *ought* to be so as part and parcel of our ontological obligation towards realizing ourselves as the sort of rational beings that can live contentedly within ourselves.[10]

The Rationale of Morality

Can morality be grounded in human nature—in some special facet or feature of our condition as rational beings? Clearly, morality does *not* inhere in the realization of human potential as such, no questions asked. For every person has a potential for *both* good and evil—in principle, each has it in them to become a saint or a sinner.

Discerning our specifically *good* potentialities requires more than a knowledge of human nature as such; it requires taking a view of the good of human beings—a normative philosophical anthropology. Of course, it is better to be healthy, to be happy, to understand what goes on, and the like. But this still leaves untouched the pivotal question of what endows life with worth and value—what are the conditions that make for a rewarding and worthwhile life? This issue of humans flourishing will inevitably involve such things as: using one's intelligence, developing (some of) one's productive talents and abilities, making a constructive contribution to the world's work, fostering the good potential of others, achieving and diffusing happiness, and taking heed for the interests of others. The good potentialities, in sum, are exactly those in whose cultivation and development a rational agent can take reflective self-satisfaction, those which help us most fully to realize ourselves as the sort of being we should ideally aspire to be. And it is here that morality's insistence on a concern for the legitimate interests of others can find a grip. The crux is simply the matter of cultivating legitimate interests. And we cannot do this for ourselves without due care for cultivating our specifically positive potentialities—those things that are inherently worthwhile.

This approach to deontology thus ultimately grounds the obligatoriness of moral injunctions in axiology—in considerations of value. For it is the metaphysics of value—and not moral theory per se—that teaches us that, other things being equal, knowledge is better than ignorance, or pleasure than pain, or compassion than needless indifference. And what ultimately validates our moral concern for the interests of others is just exactly this ontological commitment to the enhancement of value, a commitment that is inseparably linked to our own value as free rational agents.

We ought to be moral because we ought not lose out on the opportunities for realizing the positive good put at our disposal by our condition in the world's scheme of things. Immorality is wasteful and foolish, and foolishness is a betrayal of the intelligence that fate accords us.

We are embarking here on a broadly economic approach—but one that proceeds in terms of a value theory that envisions a generalized "economy of values" and from whose standpoint the traditional economic values (the standard economic costs and benefits) are merely a rather special case. Such an axiological approach sees moral rationality as an integral component of that wider rationality that calls for the effective deployment of limited resources. (Observe that such a deontological approach contrasts starkly with a utilitarian morality, in that the latter pivots morality on *happiness* or "utility" but the former on *value enhancement.*)

Heeding the strictures of morality is thus part and parcel of a rational being's cultivation of the good. For us rational creatures, morality (the due care for the interests of rational beings) is an integral component of reason's commitment to the enhancement of value. Reason's commitment to the value of rationality accordingly carries a commitment to morality in its wake. The obligatoriness of morality ultimately takes root in an *ontological* imperative to value realization with respect to the self and the world that is incumbent on free agents as such. With this ontological perspective, the ultimate basis of moral duty is rooted in the obligation we have as rational agents (towards ourselves and the world at large) to make the most and best of our opportunities for self-development. For those who might ask, "Why cultivate the things that certainly have value?" the answer is, because it is the rational thing to do.

And so, in the final analysis, one ought to be moral for the same sort of reason one ought to make use of life's opportunities in general—one's intelligence, for example, or one's other constructive talents. For in failing to do this, we throw away chances to make something of ourselves by way of contributing to the world's good, thereby failing to realize our potential. The violation of moral principles thus stands coordinate with wanton wastefulness of any sort. The crux is not so much self-realization as self-optimization, and what is at issue with failure is not merely a loss but a violation of duty as well. To recognize something as valuable is, with the rational person, to enter into certain obligations in its regard (such as favoring it over contrary alternatives, other things equal).

To be sure, it must be stressed that the obligation to morality—to conduct our interpersonal affairs appropriately by heeding the interests of others—is our only ontological obligation. The epistemic obligation to conduct our cognitive affairs appropriately—to inquire, to broaden our knowledge, to pursue the truth by believing only those things that *ought* (epistemically deserve) to be believed in the circumstances—is another example and the Kantian duty to develop (at least some of) one's talents yet another. The scope of ontological obligation is thus substantially broader than that of morality alone.

The obligation to morality, like the obligation to rationality, accordingly takes root in considerations of ontology—of our condition as the sorts of rational beings we are (or at any rate see ourselves as being). If one is in a position to see oneself as in fact rational and recognizes the value of this rationality, then one must also acknowledge the obligation to make use of one's rationality. And if one is a rational free agent who recognizes and prizes this very fact, then one ought for that very reason to behave morally by taking the interests of other such agents into account. For if I am (rationally) to pride myself on being a rational agent, then I must stand ready to value in other rational agents what I value in myself—that is, I must deem them *worthy* of respect, care, and so on in virtue of their status as rational agents. What is at issue is not so much a matter of *reciprocity* as one of *rational coherence* with claims that one does—or, rather, should—stake for oneself. To see myself in a certain normative light, I must, if rational, stand ready to view others in the same light. If we indeed are the sort of intelligent creatures whose worth in our own sight is a matter of prizing something (reflective self-respect, for example), then this item by virtue of this very fact assumes the status of something we are bound to recognize as valuable—as deserving of being valued. In seeing ourselves as *persons*—as free and responsible rational agents—we thereby rationally bind ourselves to a care for one another's interests insofar as those others too are seen as having this status.[11]

I may *desire* respect (be it self-respect or the respect of others) for all sorts of reasons, good, bad, or indifferent. But if I am to *deserve* respect, this has to be so for good reasons. Respect will certainly not come to me just because I am me, but only because I have a certain sort of respect-evoking feature (for example, being a free rational agent) whose possession (by me or, for that matter, anyone) provides a warrant for respect. And this means that *all* who have this feature (all rational agents) merit respect. Our self-worth hinges on the worth we attach to others like us: we can only have worth by virtue of possessing worth-engendering features that operate in the same way when others are at issue. To claim worthiness of respect for myself, I must concede it to all suitably constituted others as well. The first-person plural idea of "we" and "us" that projects one's own identity into a wider affinity community of rational beings is a crucial basis of our sense of worth and self-esteem. And so, in degrading other *persons* in thought or in treatment, we would automatically degrade ourselves, while in doing them honor we thereby honor ourselves.

When someone acts immorally towards me—cheats me or deceives me or the like—I am not merely angry and upset because my personal interests have been impaired, but I am also "righteously indignant." Not only has the offender failed to acknowledge me as a person (a fellow rational being with rights and interests of his own), but they have, by their very act, marked themselves as someone who, though (to my mind) a congener of mine as a rational agent, does not give us rational agents their proper due, thereby degrading the entire group to which I too belong. He has added insult to injury. And this holds true more generally. One is also indignant at witnessing someone act immorally towards a third party—being disturbed in a way that is akin to the annoyance one feels when some gaffe is committed by a member of one's own family. One's own sense of self and self-worth is mediated by membership in such a group and this can become compromised by *their* behavior. As rational agents, we are entitled and committed to be indignant at the wicked actions of our fellows who do not act as rational agents ought to because our own self-respect is inextricably bound up with their behavior. They have "let down the side."

The upshot of such considerations is that to fail to be moral is to defeat our own proper purposes and to lose out on our ontological opportunities. It is only by acknowledging the worth of others—and thus the appropriateness of a due heed of *their* interests—that we ourselves can maintain our own claims to self-respect and self-worth. And so, we realize that we *should* act morally in each and every case, even where deviations are otherwise advantageous, because insofar as we do not, we can no longer look upon ourselves in a certain sort of light—one that is crucial to our own self-respect in the most fundamental way. Moral agency is an essential requisite for the proper self-esteem of a rational being. To fail in this regard is to injure oneself where it does and should hurt the most—in one's own sight.

The ontological imperative to capitalize on our opportunities for the good carries us back to the salient issue of philosophical anthropology—the visualization of what humans can and should be. Being an "authentic human being" comes down to this: do your utmost to become the sort of rational and responsible creature that a human being, at best or most, is capable of being.[12] The moral project of treating other people as we ourselves would be treated is part and parcel of this. What we have here is in fact an evaluative metaphysics of morals.

10

By Whose Standards?

Retrospective Condemnation

How far do our ethical and evaluative standards reach across the divides of space and time? Can we appropriately judge people remote from our own setting by the criteria we would apply locally, in our own spatiotemporal proximity?

This discussion will argue against "presentism" and "localism"— the idea that we should judge others by our own standards and that our norms project all-embracingly across the reaches of time and place.

One of the many problematic aspects of the "political correctness" that has become so fashionable in this turn of the century is the tendency to condemn and disparage various individuals or groups from earlier eras for having values, opinions, and customs that our own times do not approve. The myriad available examples include:

- Condemning the Founding Fathers for their acceptance of slavery
- Condemning the politicians of the 1890–1920 era for their resistance to women's suffrage

- Condemning the industrialists of the nineteenth century for their willingness to employ child labor

Everyone will agree that people should not be inappropriately exploited, but is indentured service inappropriate exploitation? Everyone will agree that all serious stakeholders should have a say in public affairs, but are those who, like women and children, owe the state neither taxes nor military service serious stakeholders? Everyone will agree that children should not be exploited, but is offering them a chance to contribute to their family through gainful employment exploitation? There is always a gap between high-level principles and concrete conditions that leaves room for further questions.

And in this regard, a case can be made for rejecting the practice of assessing the actions and agents of the past by our own standards. For adjudging their ethical standing and moral status as good or bad, benign or evil, in the light of our current standards is something highly problematic from the angle of rationality and questionable from that of justice.

Norms and Belief

How, after all, could we reasonably expect people of distant times and places to adopt our practices and conform to our standards? The condemnation of eighteenth-century agents for failing to act on twenty-first-century ethical norms makes about as much sense as reproving eighteenth-century generals for failing to employ twenty-first-century strategies or judging medieval cartographers by twentieth-century norms.

In this regard, one cannot but heed the parallelism between the cognitive and the evaluative situation. Clearly, we cannot reproach the physicists of the eighteenth century for not employing twentieth-century standards and practices, nor even lay fault at the door of the physician of a decade ago for not conforming to the norms that subsequent discovery has made standard at the present.

Of course they could and did see matters differently because they viewed them from a different angle of vision—one that is different from ours because ours was simply not available to them.

A look at the intellectual landscape of these times shows all too clearly that many of us are deeply enmeshed in a normative egocentrism that leads us to view those of earlier times, who do not share the "enlightened" standards of our day, as being if not willfully evil then at least ethically blind. As many see it, the benighted folk of the past must simply have realized that it is wrong to exclude women from the vote, Asians from the immigration quota, Jews from the social clubs, homosexuals from military service, and the like. How can they have failed to see that inequality is unfair and ipso facto wicked?

And of course if those discriminatory practices were no more than unreasoned prejudice this view would be entirely correct. But that is assuredly not how it was. Be it right or wrong, those "wicked malefactors" of the past had, or thought they had, perfectly good reasons for their discriminatory practices—reasons that to them seemed every bit as good as our excluding child abusers from schoolmasters' posts or alcoholics from bus driving. For the most part, at least, they acted not out of an unthinking antagonism to these groups, but out of a conviction that allowing them entry into those prohibited categories would be significantly harmful to legitimate social interests. On the whole, their mind-set was not evil and their motives were not—or need not have been—outright wicked. They acted under the guidance of the good (*sub ratione boni*). They may have been—and doubtless were—mistaken in those beliefs, but even so the fact remains that the faults at issue were of intellect and understanding, not of character. And it is no more valid to reprehend such past misunderstandings than it would be to reprehend the misunderstandings of the eighteenth-century physicians who sought to treat gout by salt cures.

Who Appointed Us as Arbiter?

After all, who or what has appointed us as the supreme arbiter? Where is it written that our own standards are universally authoritative? We look down our ethical noses at these benighted legislators of seventeenth-century England who mandated drastic penalties for such minor offenses as petty theft. But where will we ourselves stand in the sight of a posterity that may well come to regard our practices in regard to abortion as nothing but casual infanticide? Our own standards should of course be seen as compelling for us—for evaluating what we ourselves and our contemporaries do here and now. If we did not see them in this light, then they just would not be "our standards." But with what right or justification can we see them as compelling for other times and places? How could we validate a normative egocentrism that elevates our present standards of judgment to a position of universal supremacy? What justifies a normative Ptolemaicism that puts us at the center of the evaluative universe?

The Agent, the Act, and the Action

A pivotal distinction must be heeded here, namely that between the moral assessment of a generic sort of act on the one hand, and on the other hand its performance in the particular action of a particular agent on a particular occasion. The questions, "Should we approve someone's performing that action here and now?" and "Should one think ill of someone who performed the action then and there?" pose very different issues—and they require different answers. Consider polygamy. Clearly we do—quite rightly—see it is a wrongful and unacceptable practice. But by this we do—or should—mean to condemn its performance here and now by people of this time and place in our own existential setting. We would and should quite properly condemn someone among our contemporary neighbors who commits this type of act. But it would certainly be morally obtuse of us if we were to comparatively condemn the biblical Abraham. Our disapproval of polygamy cannot reasonably be directed at *his* polygamy simply because the conditions and circumstances of its occurrence—the setting of circumstances and values in which it occurred—was utterly different from our own and relates to evaluative considerations that this patriarch did not and could not have had any inkling of at all. We can and should judge the abstract practice—the generic mode of action—by our own standards and according to our own lights. But this proceeds at the generic level of the abstract, not at the specific level of the concrete, and there it is only sensible and just to judge remote agents and acts by their standards—those that prevail in their particular settings and circumstances. Accordingly, we can—and should—disapprove of those acts in general without thereby derogating those remote agents and impugning their morals.

An important theoretical distinction is called for. In evaluating general practice, it is only right and proper that we should do so by our own lights—our own standards and values, those that we take ourselves to be proper and correct. But in evaluating the actions of people of another time and place, we should manifest urbanity, avoiding the parochialism of imposing our own standards and be willing to apply those of the agent's own time and place. After all, different issues are at stake, and here, as elsewhere, different questions can require different answers.

What Can Reasonably Be Expected?

When engaged in evaluating the moral or ethical condition of someone from another time and place, it is only sensible to ask: "What is reasonable to expect of this individual?" And obviously that they should conform to the norms and values of *our* place and time is simply *not* a reasonable expectation. How could those remote individuals possibly be expected to adopt and conform to those as yet unarticulated values and unknown standards? Where are they to get a crystal ball that would enable them to discern the substantially indiscernible evaluative future?

We can, in principle, operate in matters of judgment and evaluation in relation to the action and merits of people who are remote in time and setting in terms of

1. *our own* personal standards
2. the general standards of *our* time and place (our social context)
3. the general standards of *their* time and place (their social context).

Here, (2) is unsuitable because it would require people to act on the basis of considerations entirely outside the scope of their knowledge and understanding. And (1) is inappropriate both for the same reason, and because it asks of people more than could ever reasonably be expected of them. For only (3)—the one and only remaining alternative—is practicable in this connection. For only the abstract act can rightly be judged by us according to our own standards and not its performance by some remote agents. To make one's moral assessment of the people and actions of another place and time in line with one's own values and standards is to proceed in a way that is clearly parochial, urbanity deficient, and narrow-minded. And it is also unjust because it calls for expecting of someone something that they could not possibly manage to achieve. We might perhaps hope that people will look beyond the baseline of a normative localism, and we would certainly welcome their doing so, but we have no right to expect it of them.

That the reach of one's obligations do not outrun the limits of the possible has been a legal maxim since Roman times (*Ultra posse nemo obligatur*). And at the base of the matter lies the issue of rationality. After all, it is absurd to ever ask for something that exceeds the limits of the possible. And exactly this principle regarding legal obligation holds good for moral obligation as well. That which lies beyond a person's powers due to conditions that the conditional individual is nowise responsible for is something for which they cannot bear reasonable reprehension. Justifiable reproach stops at the limits of effective responsibility. And for this reason, if no other, applying unavailable standards would be both unreasonable and unjust.

A Kantian Perspective

As Immanuel Kant already insisted long ago, the pivotal factor in the moral assessment of an agent's actions pivots on this agent's motives for doing it.[1] The performance of even an inherently meritorious action (helping someone in need) can be reprehensible if done for an unsavory motive (seeking praise), and even an inherently wrongful action (inflicting pain on someone) can be meritorious if done for a benign motive (saving his life in a medical procedure). And while loyalty to the values and practices of our time and place is in ordinary circumstances appropriate and thereby should in general motivate *our* actions, those of the agents of the past are going to depend on the norms of *their* day because only these norms can possibly play a role in their motivation.

What is inappropriate about judging people and their acts by standards other than their own is that these are not *available* to them. Only the norms of their time and place are accessible to individuals and able to canalize their doings and dealings. It is inappropriate to bring other norms to bear because it is irrational to demand that an agent should govern their doings by considerations outside their ken.

When considering what we take to be the misdeeds of the people of other times and places we are certainly entitled

- to disapprove of what they thought and did, and
- to regret that they did it

But we are not comparably entitled

- to condemn them for the thinking and doing of it.

We must in this context keep in view a clear separation between the act and the agent, and we cannot automatically transmute disapproval of the act into condemnation of the agent.

To justly engage the actions of an agent we have to take that agent's thought and motives into account. And when looking at what we disapprove of in the deeds of people of other places and times, we often cannot get around the fact that—to put it crudely—they just didn't know any better. An agent of the past no more deserves automatic condemnation as wicked for doing something that we would deem so in our contemporaries than a savant of the past would deserve condemnation for beliefs we would regard as inappropriate and uninformed in a scientist of our day.

It is not only right but inevitable that one must judge *our* issues by *our* standards (they would not be our standards if we did otherwise). How then could we in all fairness deny a like privilege to others?

The Role of Our Standards

An important distinction must be introduced at this point, however. Up to this stage we have simply spoken of "standards" indiscriminately, as though all standards were created equal. But this is certainly not the case. There are standards and then there are standards. And in particular, there are standards of *adequacy* and standards of *excellence*. Any and every apparatus of evaluation permits of distinctions along these qualitative lines as between norms for run-of-the-mill performance and norms for superior performance.

Of others we are, by rights, entitled to expect in moral and ethical matters no more than adequate performance. Here, we have to satisfy ourselves with gray mediocrity. With others, doing more than this is a matter of supererogation as far as we ourselves are concerned. Only of ourselves are we entitled—indeed obligated—to demand superior performance, of others we can reasonably expect no more than mere adequacy.

But on what comparative basis can this ordinary/superior distinction be predicated? Of course it will have to be that of the general cast of characters that populate "their world." That is to say we must judge them—those remote agents—by the generally prevalent standards of their time and place. Only where that time and place is our own and the people at issue are ourselves are we entitled to view those general standards in a critical spirit and to ask for more—for ethically superior performance. The rest we must judge on the basis of their doing when in Rome that which the Romans do. To ask more of them would be to ask for too much—and the error here would be ours.

Because motivation plays so pivotal a role in moral appraisal, all that we can properly expect of someone in matters of ethical assessment is that they should act in accordance with the values and standards of their time and place. And that is all that we can reasonably expect of our own contemporaries and neighbors as well. *Only of ourselves can we justifiably expect more.* Here we can and should demand excellence rather than adequacy. In relation to our own actions we should *not* see the standards of our place and time as necessarily binding because we have the (moral) obligation to assess the appropriateness and validity of these standards themselves, and we should not see them as gift horses that we should not expect to scrutinize. But with others the matter is different. While we have a special sort of standing and responsibility towards ourselves, this is not so with them.

It is, of course, every person's right—nay, duty—to do what they can to ensure that the general standards of their environment are excellent rather than mediocre, and manifest an impetus to high quality rather than (as seems to be the case in our own place and time) dropping through the floor to mediocrity and "going to hell in a handbasket." But this aspect of one's own moral duty is not the point of our present concerns, which address the ethical and moral assessment of remote agents. And here in the absence of specific, case-characterizing information as to their intentions and motives, we must and should conform our assessment to the standards of the place and time. Thus when it comes to approving or disapproving the actions and character of people, the pertinent apparatus of standards of judgment and evaluation will have to be that of their setting, and it will only be in a very special close to home case (that is, when dealing with ourselves) that we are rationally and ethically entitled to ask for more.

On Rendering Justice

In judging people by the standards of their time and place, we do of course have to reckon with the fact that those standards may be seriously deficient from our own evaluative point of view. But nevertheless, the fact remains that if the standards allotted to them by their historico-cultural setting were deficient (as we ourselves see it), then this is something for which we cannot very well blame them—any more than whatever reproach may ultimately be seen to be deserved by the standards of our time and place can be imputed to any one of us. The deficiency of their standards is not their fault but rather their loss. It is no valid basis for reproaching someone in the context of moral appraisal, but it is something for which the individual is more to be pitied than censured.

The only fair and reasonable course to take in matters of moral evaluation is to judge people in terms of what they did with the opportunities at their disposal—how they played the hand that fate dealt to them. In evaluating the acts or morals of someone of another place or time, our obligation (by our own standards and values) is surely to render justice and fairness to those with whom we deal. And only by judging them against the background of their own values and standards can we manage to accord them their fairness and justice that is the right of all.

A Key Objection

"But what if those standards and values of the place and time are transparently evil and malign by our own standards—those which alone we can accept as being appropriate? What of the value system of Hitler's Germany or Stalin's USSR? Are such monstrous value systems to be accepted as furnishing usable norms?"

The first question to be asked here is whether it is indeed the case that these malign norms were indeed "the values of the time and place"—that is, mid-twentieth-century Europe. In addressing that question of time and place, we must not draw our borders too narrowly so as to elevate local eccentricities into cultural norms.

The pivotal question when judging those "wrongdoers of the past" is not, "Should they (ideally) have known better?" but rather, "Could they (realistically) have known better?" And the consideration that leads us rightly to condemn the sundry, egregious malefactors who constitute a prime example here (Polish pogromists, Stalinist executioners, Nazi gauleiters, and the like) is that they could and should have known better—and usually doubtless did so, as their efforts to conceal their actions proves. On this basis, the consideration that renders the treatment of the Amerindians by the conquistadors particularly contemptible is the prominent presence among them of numerous friars who did their utmost to provide them of ample opportunity "to know better." But whenever we cannot construct a case for holding that these "malefactors" of other times and places did in fact have such an opportunity, it is neither reasonable nor just to reprehend them.

Relativism Rejected

"Judge the actions of people by the standards of their place and time." But isn't that just bad old relativism?

This, of course, will very much depend on just what it is that one takes to be at issue with "relativism." Now, standardly, this is construed as a mode of indifferentism: you just pick your standards and to each his own—it just doesn't matter. And this, of course, is emphatically not what is being maintained here. Such indifferentism is not even at issue here because the value and standards of one's place and time are not matters of free choice to individuals; they are situational givens, not deliberated options. What is contemplated here is accordingly not an indifferentist relativism, but rather the contextualism of a situationally determinate value system. This point deserves a somewhat closer look.

The reality of it is that no system, of specific beliefs, of concrete value, or of moral norms is an extramundane absolute, mandated in unchangeable perfection by the abstract nature of things. The best we can do is to figure things out by our own lights. And here we can do no more than make use of the local, particularized, diversified instruments that we humans can manage to develop within the sociocultural limitations of our place and time. Thus far, contextualism is both inevitable and correct. This situation emphatically does *not* engender an indifferentist and subjectivist relativism. The crucial point is that one can be a contextualistic pluralist in matters of morality without succumbing to such indifferentist relativism (let alone nihilistic skepticism).

The characteristic flaw of relativism is its insistence on the *rational indifference* of alternatives. Be it contentions, beliefs, doctrines, practices, customs, or whatever is at issue, the relativist insist that "it just doesn't matter" in point of rationality. People are led to adopt one alternative over another by *extra-rational* considerations (custom, habituation, fashion, or whatever); from the rational point of view there is nothing to choose—all the alternatives stand on the same footing. Presented with alternatives of the sort at issue—be it cognitive, moral, or whatever—the relativist insists that at bottom it just doesn't matter—at any rate as far as the rationality of the issue is concerned. The fatal flaw of this position is rooted in the fact that our claims, beliefs, doctrines, practices, customs, all belong to identifiable departments of purposive human endeavor—identifiable domains, disciplines, and the like. For all (or virtually all) human enterprises are at bottom teleological—conducted with some sort of end or objective in view.

Now in this context, the crucial fact is that some claims, beliefs, doctrines, practices, customs, and so on are bound to serve the purposes of their domain better than others. For it is pretty much inevitable that in any goal-oriented enterprise, some alternative ways of proceeding serve better than others with respect to the relevant range of purpose, proving more efficient and effective in point of goal-realization. And in the teleological contexts, they *thereby* establish themselves as rationally appropriate with respect to the issues. It lies in the nature of the thing that the quintessentially rational thing to do is to give precedence and priority to those alternatives that are more effective with respect to the range of purposes at issue.

Moral absolutism is to be rejected because a moral code is in its details not a matter of one size fits all uniformity.[2] But equally, moral indifferentism is to be rejected because the moral code of one's own community has a valid claim to our allegiance, barring any specific and cogent reasons to the contrary. We thus reject relativism in favor of an objectivism that sees objectivity not as a matter of a "God's eye view" but rather one that we ourselves can see as reasonable insofar as we are being reasonable about the pursuit of our own projects.

Hoisted by One's Own Petard?

A subtle and sophisticated objection looms up at this point:

> You say it is inappropriate and ethically obtuse to judge the people of another day and place by the standards of our own. And you say that instead they should be judged by the standards of their own time and place. But then look to our own contemporaries—the people of *our* time and place. As you yourself say, they seem to be given to judging everyone by their standards—past people included. If it indeed is nowadays a normal practice to judge the past by current standards, then how can you possibly condemn this practice? After all, you insist that we can expect no more of people than of conformity to the norms of their place and time. In line with your own principles, you should therefore see this as only to be expected and refrain from disapproval on this basis.

However, this subtle and sophisticated objection is no better than sophistical. It fails to take heed of the distinction, carefully drawn above, between evaluating a generic mode of acting on the one hand, and on the other hand, evaluating a particular agent's actions. We can condemn a mode of acting and yet see it in certain circumstances as understandable and venial. It is not being maintained that those critics and commentators who engage in criticizing past actions and agents by current standards deserve condemnation. We can and should be liberal towards them and understanding towards their actions. But what we need not and should not do is to approve of the agents' actions at issue. Here, as elsewhere, we can—and should—be understanding of the wrongdoer without endorsing the wrongdoing.

How, after all, would we ourselves want to be judged by our posterity—what would we regard proper and appropriate here? Think of an example. Consider abortion—especially after the first trimester. It is perfectly conceivable (I don't say likely) that the sensibilities of a later age will look on this as a form of murder—pretty much as we ourselves view the "exposure" of unwanted baby girls in rural China. Surely we would resent the idea that the mothers of these potential children should be adjudged to be murderesses. Nor would we approve of condemnation if there came a time when people came to view automobile driving as a barbaric and callously life-indifferent practice, because we know full well in advance that hundreds of lives will be sacrificed on its altar over every holiday weekend.

The Demands of Rationality and Justice

The salient point of these deliberations is that moral evaluation is itself a mode of activity that is inevitably subject to moral standards. Passing moral and ethical judgment on people and their acts is itself an ethically laden step that has direct implications for our own moral standing. For doing this is something that we can do more or less justly, more or less fairly, more or less conscientiously. Thus in engaging in this generic practice, we ourselves are doing something that has an ethical dimension. As the Bible tells us, in judging others we lay ourselves open to judgment.

While those doings of the people of others times and places is a matter of what *they* did, our forming evaluative judgments about this is a matter of what *we ourselves* are doing. And as such, this process of evaluative appraisal regarding people's doings has a pervasively ethical coloration. And accordingly, it can—and should—be asked of us that we have proceeded in an ethically appropriate way, proceeding with a view to such salient, here and now pertinent factors of evaluative property as *fairness, justice, reasonableness,* urbanity, and generosity. The evaluative practice we are concerned with falls within the scope of its own concerns. It is something in which the interests of others are engaged in a way that demands procedural appropriateness on our part.

Accordingly, we here have both the right and the obligation to require and achieve an at least adequate level of ethical performance in assessing people's judgmental practices. And the demands of adequacy in this context take heed of those salient values that have just been enumerated. At this second level removed, it is indeed those standards that are—or should be—ours that are determinative. But in this regard, evaluating the acts and merits of people of other times and places by the current standards of the present (let alone by our own personal standards) is unfair, unreasonable, unjust, ungenerous, and unrealistic.

In the final analysis, this business of evaluating others is something that we ourselves conduct on our own account, and thereby is bound to be something that is—or should be—subject to *our* norms. And so, what is now at issue calls for applying our standards to what we ourselves are doing here and now. And here the operative norms of justice and fairness that hold for us call for reliance on *their* norms in forming our judgments regarding them. It is our own values that do—and should—cry out loud for evaluating those of other places and times by *their* standards rather than *ours*.

Thus in this matter of second-level considerations—of the standards governing *our own* evaluative practice—it is indeed *our* standards that should be operative. And the demand that these standards make upon our evaluative modus operandi is that it shall proceed with reference to the standards of the subjects of evaluation (rather than those of the evaluating agent). In this regard, the prime directive alike of reasonableness and justice is represented by the commandment, "By the standards of their day shall ye judge them."

11

Pluralism and Concretization Quandaries

The Question of Political Consensus

Is seeking consensus to be regarded as a prime imperative of rational social policy? To be sure, the widely favored allocation of a pride of place to consensus sounds benevolent, irenic, and socially delectable. Indeed, it may sound so plausible at first that it is difficult to see how a person of reasonableness and goodwill could fail to go along. Nevertheless, there is room for real doubt as to whether this utopian-sounding position makes sense. Serious questions can be raised as to whether the best interests of a healthy community are served by a commitment to consensus.

In and of itself, consensus is clearly no absolute. One obviously has to worry about what it is that people are in consensus about and why it is they are so. (Think of the precedent of Nazi Germany.) All the same, the idea has been astir in some European intellectual circles for many years now that a just and democratic society can be achieved only on the basis of a shared social commitment to the pursuit of communal consensus. Such a view insists that the public harmony required for the smooth functioning of a benign social order must be rooted in an agreement on fundamentals. Progress toward a congenial and enlightened society accordingly requires an unfolding course of evolving consensus about the public agenda—a substantial agreement regarding the practical question of what is to be done.

This general line of thought traces back to Hegel, who envisioned an inexorable tendency towards a condition of things where all thinking people will share a common acceptance of the manifold of truths revealed by reason. Sailing in Hegel's wake, the tradition of German social thought, reaching through Marx to the Frankfurt School and beyond, has reinforced the idea that the realization of a communally benign social order requires a commitment to consensus—a shared public commitment to the idea that the pursuit of consensus in communal affairs is a great and good thing.

This position, however, is deeply problematic. A good case can be made out for the contrary view that a benign social order need not be committed to the quest for consensus but can be constituted along very different, irreducibly *pluralistic* lines. After all, the idea that a consensus on fundamentals is realistically available is in fact false with respect to most large, complex, advanced societies and is simply not needed for the benign and "democratic" management of communal affairs. And even the idea that consensus is a desirable ideal is very questionable.

To begin at the end, let it be foreshadowed that the policy whose appropriateness will be defended here is one of a *restrained dissonance* based on an acceptance of a diversity and dissensus (disagreement, discord) of opinion—a benevolent (or at any rate resigned) acceptance of the disagreement of others with a credo of respect to beliefs and values. Such an approach envisions a posture of diversity conjoined with "live and let live," taking the line that a healthy democratic social order can not only tolerate but even—within limits—welcome dissensus, provided that the conflicts involved are kept within "reasonable bounds." The present discussion will accordingly maintain the merits of the consensus-dispensing view that a benign social order can be unabashedly pluralistic and based not on the pursuit of agreement but on arrangements that provide for *acquiescence in disagreement.* This position sees as perfectly acceptable a situation that is not one of judgmental homogeneity and uniformity, but one of a dissonance and diversity that is restrained to a point well short of outright conflict and chaos.

Dissensus has this to be said for it, at least: it is at odds with a stifling orthodoxy. A dissent-accommodating society is ipso facto pluralistic, with all the advantages that accrue in situations where no one school of thought is able to push the others aside. Indeed, the extent to which a society exhibits tolerance—is willing and able to manage a consensual diversity arising from free thought and expression—could be seen as a plausible standard of merit, since a spirit of mutual acceptance and accommodation is one of the hallmarks of a benign and productive social order.

It must be acknowledged, of course, that dissensus does have a negative side. Its negativities preeminently include:

1. The danger of escalation from productive competition to destructive conflict.

2. The possible diversion of resources (effort and energy) into potentially unproductive forms of rivalry.

3. The separatist fragmentation of the community into groups estranged from each other in a posture of mutual hostility.

4. The tendency to dismiss otherwise meritorious plans, projects, and ideas simply because they originate from the "outside," from a rival, competing source.

Clearly, the story is not altogether one-sided. However, situations where the public good is best served by a general acquiescence in disagreement are not only perfectly possible but also often actual. Life being what it is, it would be too hard on all of us to be in a position where we had to reach agreement in matters of opinion and evaluation. A society in which the various schools of thought and opinion try to win the others over by rational suasion is certainly superior to one in which they seek to do so by force or intimidation. But this does not automatically make it superior to one where these groups let one another alone to flourish or flounder in their divergent individuality.

Acquiescence and Controlled Conflict

Consensus by its very nature is a condition of intellectual uniformity, the homogeneity of thought and opinion. And just herein lie some of its significant shortcomings. For the fact is that the impulsion to consensus will in various circumstances prove itself to be:

1. An impediment to creativity and innovation. (Settling into consensus is a discouragement from endeavoring to outdo others and striving to improve on their efforts by "doing one's utmost to excel.")

2. An invitation to mediocrity. (By its very nature, the realization of consensus involves a compromise among potentially divergent tendencies. Thus, it tends to occupy "the middle ground" where people are most easily brought together, but where, for that very reason, the element of creative, insightful innovation is likely to be missing.)

3. A disincentive to productive effort. (One of the most powerful motives for improving the level of one's performance is, after all, to come under the pressure of competition and the threat of being outdone by a rival.)

Not only is insistence on the pursuit of general consensus in practical matters and public affairs unrealistic, it is also counterproductive. For it deprives us of the productive stimulus of competition and the incentive of rivalry. In many situations of human life, people are induced to make their best effort in inquiry or creative activity through rivalry rather than emulation, through differentiation rather than conformity, through an attempt to impede the folly they see all around. Productivity, creativity, and the striving for excellence are—often as not—the offspring of diversity and conflict.

Most human intellectual, cultural, and social progress has begun with an assault by dissident spirits against a comfortably established consensus. The Andalusian friar, Bartolomeo de las Casas, upheld the human rights of Amerindians against the consensus of Spanish conquistadores and settlers alike that they were inferior beings; the eighteenth-century American abolitionists protested the institution of slavery in the teeth of a vast preponderance of powerful opponents; J. S. Mill's protest against "the subjection of women" was a lone voice crying out in a wilderness of vociferous males. And lest it be said that such "eccentric" but benevolent views did all eventually win through a general consensus of thought and universality of practice, one can point to the teaching of Jesus whose widespread endorsement is largely a matter of words and not deeds. We can have no comfortable assurance about the present—or future—consensual victory of truth, justice, and the cause of rightness.

When we find ourselves dissenting from others, we may dislike their opinions and disapprove of their actions—and they of ours—but we can, by and large, manage to come to terms. We can—often, at least—"get along" with others quite adequately when we can "agree to disagree" or when we can simply ignore, dismiss, and sideline our disagreements, postponing further opposition for another day. What matters for social harmony is not that we agree with one another, but that each of us acquiesces in what the other is doing, that we "live and let live," so we avoid letting our differences become a casus belli between *us*. Acquiescence is the key. And this is not a matter of *approbation*, but rather one of a mutual restraint that, even when disapproving and disagreeing, is willing (no doubt reluctantly) to "let things be," because the alternative—actual conflict or warfare—will lead to a situation that is still worse. All is well as long as we can manage to keep our differences beneath the threshold of outright conflict.

The crucial fact about *acquiescence* is that it is generally rooted not in *agreement* with others but rather in a preparedness to get on without it. What makes good practical and theoretical sense is the step of (on occasion) accepting something without agreeing with it—of "going along" despite disagreement—an acquiescence of diversity grounded in a resigned toleration of the discordant views of others. The merit of such tolerance is not (as John Stuart Mill had it) that it is an interim requisite for progress toward an ultimate, collective realization of the truth, but simply and less ambitiously, that it is a requisite for the peace and quiet that we all require for the effective pursuit of our own varied visions and projects.

Historical experience, empirical understanding of the human realities, and theoretical analysis of our social situation all conjoin to indicate that an insistence on agreement among rational inquirers and problem-solving agents is simply futile. However inconvenient for philosophers, ample experience shows that not only in matters of politics, art, and religion but also in a whole host of cognitive domains like history, economics, social science, and philosophy, we shall never actually achieve a firmly-secured general consensus. And there is no reason to think that a benign society can exist only where the clash of private opinions and preferences is extinguished by the processes of social coordination. A healthy social order can perfectly well be based not on agreement but on the sort of mutual restraint in which subgroups simply go their own way—live and let live—in the face of dissensus.

Neither in intellectual nor in social contexts, after all, have we any firm assurance that a consensual position somehow represents the objectively correct or operationally optimal solution. To be sure, in many cases some sort of resolution must be arrived at with respect to public issues. But we need not *agree* about it: a perfectly viable result may be had simply on the basis of a reluctant acceptance of diversity. What matters for the smooth functioning of a social order is not that the individuals or groups that represent conflicting positions should think alike, but simply that they acquiesce in certain shared ways of conducting the society's affairs.

Concretization Quandaries

Consensus polity has practical as well as theoretical weaknesses. A concretization quandary arises when it is a good idea to do A, but the only way to do so concretely is by doing A_1 or A_2 or A_3, and so on, while nevertheless doing each of these A_i is a bad idea. In such situations there is no concrete way of realizing a generically desirable objective.

There are innumerable cases in which the democratic process so operates that a social program or public work is generally acknowledged as something that is abstractly (or generically) desirable, but where nevertheless each and every one of the concrete ways of realizing it is deemed unacceptable. In such a situation, our mini-society finds itself in a *concretization quandary*: there is no majority accepted way of reaching a majority accepted goal. This general phenomenon is, after all, often encountered in the political arena, where we frequently read in the press stories of the following tendency:

> When asked what congress should do about the Federal deficit, two-thirds of the voters preferred cuts in major spending programs, but this support for spending cuts dissipated whenever it came to specific programs.

We have here a perplexity that is only too common in democratic political contexts. Think of the common situation of a congressional stalemate or gridlock where there is a virtually overwhelming public pressure—duly recognized in congress—that something be done to resolve a certain problem, while nevertheless each of the available solutions is deemed unacceptable. We confront *gridlock* whenever various interest groups manage to vitiate a general agreement that something be done with some combination of the groups managing to defeat each one of the concretizations of that generally agreed desideratum. In such situations, every *available* solution generates an opposition sufficiently powerful to defeat it. The upshot here defeats the plausible principle that "to will the end is to will the means," because each and every one of the means to that accepted end is itself deemed unacceptable.

Such concretization quandaries reflect the *logical* impracticability of adopting the pervasive and seemingly natural principle of the (seemingly) democratic process: *majorities represent the will of the group; if the majority wants it done, then so be it—let it be done.* For in various cases, the majority indeed wants something to be done. Yet, this end can only be achieved by adopting one or another concrete implementing measure, and a majority is against doing each and every one of these individual concretizations—with the result of "gridlocking" that universally favored measure. Only by somehow forming a particular result in which every part at least acquiesces can that generally favored objective be realized in such circumstances.

Some Objections

Consider the following line of objection put forward by a hypothetical critic:

I agree with much of what you have said on the merits of dissensus and diversity. But you have failed to reckon with the crucial distinction between a consensus on matters of ground-level *substance* and a consensus on matters of *procedure*. As you maintain, a benign social order can indeed dispense with a substantive consensus regarding *what* is decided upon. But what it indispensably requires is a procedural agreement on modes of conflict resolution—a second-order consensus about *how* those first-order issues are to be decided. If the society is to serve effectively the interests of those involved, and if mutual strife and conflict are to be averted, there must be a consensus on *process* or the validity of the procedural ways in which these base-level resolutions are arrived at. Consensus on particular decisions may be dispensable, but consensus on the decision-making *process* is essential.

Despite its surface plausibility, even this more sophisticated argument for the necessity of an at least procedural consensuality is deeply problematic.

For one thing, even where there is a consensus about process, there may nevertheless be sharp disagreement regarding matters of implementation. Even where people agree on, say maintenance of law and order, civility of interaction, an equitable distribution of resources—and many other such "procedural" principles of human action in the public domain—such procedural agreements are much too abstract to define particular public policies. (We can agree on the need for "law and order" and yet quite plausibly disagree sharply on questions of civil disobedience and the limits of appropriate protest.) Process consensus is a lot to ask for—but still is not sufficient for a benign social order.

But the problem goes even deeper. For it is simply false that procedural agreement is indispensable for a benign social order. To manage its affairs in a mutually acceptable way, a community needs no agreement on the merits of those procedures as long as there is acquiescence in their operation. What matters is *not* that we agree on methods—I may have my favorite and you yours. I might, for example, think that the proper way to address the issue at hand is for the electorate to decide it by referendum; you think that the right and proper way is by a vote in the legislature. But as long as we both acquiesce in the established process of having the courts decide, then all is well. There is no *agreement* here: we emphatically do not concur in thinking that the courts are the proper (let alone the best!) avenue for a solution—in fact, *neither* of us thinks so. What we do is simply acquiesce in what the courts make their decisions on the issue. What matters for irenic conflict resolution is not second-order consensus but second-order acquiescence. A sensible defense of acquiescence is accordingly not predicated on ignoring the distinction between first-order, substantive issues and second-order, methodological ones. Rather it is prepared to turn this distinction to its own purposes and to see it as advantageous rather than inimical to establish the claims of acquiescence vis-à-vis consensus.

But even when we "agree to disagree" do we not in fact agree? Not really. Or, rather, we do so in name only! An agreement to disagree is as much an agreement as a paper dragon is a dragon—the whole point is that there is no agreement at all here. Parties who agree to disagree do not *agree* on anything—they simply exhibit a similarity of behavior in that they walk away from a disagreement. They no more agree than do bouncing billiard balls that move away from one another.

Another possible objection to an emphasis on acquiescence as a mechanism of social decision runs as follows:

> To cast acquiescence in a leading role in the management of public affairs is to invite the deployment of raw power; to open the doors to coercion, oppression, domination, and the subjection of the weak to control by the strong.

But this view of the matter is simply unjust. The rational person's acquiescence is, after all, based on a cost-benefit calculation that weighs the costs of opposition against the costs of "going along." And to deploy raw power is to raise the stakes—to readjust not only the benefits but also the costs of acquiescence. And as those who study revolutions soon learn, it is precisely at the point when power is made blatantly overt—when bayonets are mounted and blood is shed in the streets—that acquiescence is most gravely endangered.

It is clear that discernibly just, benign, and generally advantageous arrangements will secure the acquiescence of people far more readily and more extensively than those that infringe upon such obvious social desiderata. It is quite false that an approach that roots social legitimacy in acquiescence somehow favors oppression and injustice. To be sure, much will depend on the sorts of people one is dealing with. If they are unreasonably longsuffering and spineless—if they are weak-kneed and cave in easily under pressure—then a social order based on acquiescence is one in which they indeed can be oppressed and exploited. (But then, of course, if they are totally accommodating and yielding, a consensual order based on agreement with others is also one in which their true interests are likely to suffer.) The fact remains that sensible people are distinctly unlikely to acquiesce in arrangements that are oppressive to them. An acquiescence-oriented political process does not provide a rationale for domination, exploitation, and oppression precisely because these are factors in which sensible people are unlikely to acquiesce—once brought into play they soon call forth opposition rather than accommodation. One of the early lessons that an acquiescence-based society learns is that its ethics are not smoothly viable if people are constantly testing the limits of acquiescence. An emphasis on being civilized, urbane, and restrained is not at odds with acquiescence but is actually conducive to the enterprise.

Moreover, the complaint that a polity of acquiescence inherently favors the perpetration of injustices cannot be sustained. Acquiescence is like agreement in that nobody else can do it for you. People may be able to rearrange the conditions under which you will have to proceed in this regard, but how you proceed within those conditions is always in the final analysis up to you. As recent developments in Eastern Europe all too clearly show, people will only acquiesce in injustice up to a certain point. After that they turn to non-cooperation and opposition—they take up arms against the sea of troubles or perhaps simply emigrate. The limits of acquiescence are finite.

Admittedly, acquiescence can be bad—it can be forced or compelled. It is no automatic route to political legitimacy. But then of course neither is consensus. We are always entitled to ask why people agree: is it for a good and valid reason—a concern for truth or for fairness, say—or is it because of self-interest, conformism, constraint, or propagandism. Legitimacy is always an additional issue. And just as it is not just consensus one wants but a consensus that is rational and free, so it is not just acquiescence one wants but acquiescence that is given in a way that is sensible and uncoerced.

The Wider Political Perspective

A great continental divide runs across the landscape of philosophy. On the one side lies the Platonic tradition that looks to systemic order through a rational coordination under the aegis of universal principles. On the other side lies the Aristotelian tradition that looks to organic balance and an equilibration of diversity and division. The one is geared to a classicism of holistic order, the other to a pluralism of countervailing checks and balances. The one favors the rational uniformity of a harmonious consensus, the other the creative diversity of a limited dissensus. The one invokes the tidiness of theorizing reason, the other the diversified complexity of actual history.

Given this divide, European political thought since the time of the Enlightenment has been fixated upon the idea of the "general consent" of the people in defining a general agreement of the community (*la volonte generale*), which may or may not be all that apparent to the people themselves (and may need to be discerned on their behalf by some particularly insightful elite). All the same, that the dangers of this idea run amuck is apparent to anyone who has looked even casually into the history of the French Revolution.

The polity of consensus proceeds from a fundamentally socialistic commitment to the coordination and alignment of individual action into the uniform social order of "rationalized" central planning (albeit, no doubt, a uniformization that is not imposed, but rather engendered—presumably—through the "hidden hand" of an idealized rationality). Legislatures, taxing authorities, and political theorists all like to keep the affairs of the citizenry neat and tidy. But the fact of the matter is that the impetus to public consensus, agreement, and concurrence of thought will not be high on the priority list of the true friends of personal freedom and liberty. And so, the polity of pluralism abandons the goal of a monolithically unified "rational order" for the "creative diversity" of a situation of variegated rivalry and competition. Its political paradigm is not that of a command economy, with its ideal of rationalization and uniformizing coordination, but that of a free market with its competitive rivalry of conflicting interests. Consensuality looks to uniformity of thought, pluralism to reciprocally fruitful harmonization of discordant elements.

Rather different sorts of policy approaches are at work in social orders based on consensus-oriented and acquiescence-oriented principles. Consensus-seeking societies will aim to maximize the number of people who approve of what is being done; acquiescence-seeking societies seek to minimize the number of people who disapprove *very* strongly of what is being done. The one seeks actual agreement, the other seeks to avoid disagreement so keen as to preclude acquiescence. The two processes sound similar but are in actual fact quite different in spirit and in mode of operation.

The social requisite of a viable public order can thus plausibly be viewed to lie not in the formation of consensus but in the forging of conditions in which people who disagree—even on fundamentals—can nevertheless manage to acquiesce in dissensus through recognizing this as a state of affairs that is not only tolerable but even in some way beneficial. Insofar as consensus is something positive then, it has to be seen in the light of a desideratum rather than a valid aspiration of the sort at issue with an ideal. The polity of consensus is too utopian to provide us with so useful an instrument. Consensus simply is not a requisite for the prime social desideratum of having people lead lives that are at once personally satisfying and socially constructive.[1] The crux of the matter is finding and prompting arrangements that make it possible for people who disagree to nevertheless contribute to a common good.

12

The Power of Ideals

The Service of Ideals

Ideals pivot on the question, "If I could shape the world as I want, how would I have it be?" And, of course, *every* voluntary action of ours is in some manner a remaking of the world—at any rate, of a very small corner of it—by projecting into reality a situation that otherwise would not be. To act intelligently is to act with due reference to the *direction* in which our own actions shift the course of things. And this is exactly where ideals come into play. Our ideals guide and consolidate our commitment to human virtues in general and moral excellences in particular. Courage and unselfishness provide examples, seeing that they often lead beyond "the call of duty," exhibiting a dimension of morality that transcends the boundaries of obligation in a way that is typical of ideals.

In an influential 1958 paper, the English philosopher J. O. Urmson stressed the ethical importance of Christian theology's conception of works of supererogation (*opera supererogationis*),[1] reemphasizing the traditional contrast between the *basic* morality of duties and the *higher* morality of preeminently creditable action "above and beyond the call of duty." Such supererogation is best conceived of not in terms of duty but in terms of dedication to an ideal. The values at issue are often symbolized in such "role models" as heroes and saints. An ethic of ideals can accommodate what is at issue here in ways that a mere ethic of duty cannot. Nobody has a *duty* to his fellows to become a saint or hero; this just is not something we *owe* to people, be it singly or collectively. Here, we are dealing with something that is not so much a matter of actual duty as one of dedication to an ideal—the benevolent, inner impetus to make the world a better place.

There is always something unrealistic about ideals. So what are they good for? Many things. A knowledge of their ideals gives us much insight into what people do: "By their ideals shall ye know them." We get to know a great deal about someone when we know about his or her ideals—about their dreams, their heroes, and their utopias. The question of what gods somebody worships—power or fame or Mammon or Jehovah—does much to inform us about the sort of person we are dealing with. (To be sure, what we do not yet know is how *dedicated* this person to those ideals—how energetically and assiduously he or she puts them to work.)

Human aspiration is not restricted by realities—neither by the realities of the present moment (from which our sense of future possibilities can free us), nor even by our view of realistic future prospects (from which our sense of the ideal possibilities can free us). Our judgment is not bounded by what *is*, nor by what *will* be, nor even by what *can* be. There is always also our view of what *should* be. The vision of our mind's eye extends to circumstances beyond the limits of the possible. A proper appreciation of ideals calls for a recognition of man's unique dual citizenship in the worlds of the real and the ideal—a realm of facts and a realm of values.

It is remarkable that nature has managed to evolve a creature who aspires to more than nature can offer, who never totally feels at home in its province, but lives, to some extent, as an alien in a foreign land. All those who feel dissatisfied with the existing scheme of things, who both yearn *and strive* for something better and finer than this world affords, have a touch of moral grandeur in their makeup that deservedly evokes admiration.

Sceptically inclined "realists" have always questioned the significance of ideals on the grounds that, being unrealizable, they are presumably pointless. But this fails to reckon properly with the realities of the situation. For while ideals are, in a way, mere fictions, they nevertheless direct and canalize our thought and action. To be sure, an ideal is not a goal we can expect to attain. But it serves to set a direction in which we can strive. Ideals are irrealities, but they are irrealities that condition the nature of the real through their influence on human thought and action. Stalin's cynical question, "But how many divisions has the Pope?" betokens the Soviet *Realpolitiker* rather than the Marxist ideologue (how many soldiers did Karl Marx command?). It is folly to underestimate the strength of an attachment to ideals. Though in itself impracticable, an ideal can nevertheless importantly influence our praxis and serve to shape the sort of home we endeavor to make for ourselves in a difficult world.

Ideals take us beyond experience into the realm of *imagination*—outside of what we do find, or expect to find, here in this real world, it is the region of wishful thinking, of utopian aspiration, of what we would fain have if only (alas!) we could. Admittedly, this envisions a perfection or completion that outreaches not only what we actually have attained, but even what we can possibly attain in this sublunary dispensation. However, to give this up, to abandon casting those periodic wistful glances in the "transcendental" direction is to cease to be fully, genuinely, and authentically human. In following empiricists and positivists by fencing the ideal level of deliberation off behind "No Entry" signs, we diminish the horizons of human thought to its grave impoverishment. (As is readily illustrated by examples from Galileo and Einstein, there is a valid place for thought experiments that involve idealization even in the domain of the natural sciences themselves.)

The level of idealized contemplation provides a most valuable conceptual instrument, for it affords us a most useful *contrast conception* that serves to shape and condition our thought. Like the functionary imperial Rome that stood at the emperor's side to whisper intimations of mortality into his ear, so idealizations serve to remind us of the fragmentary, incomplete, and parochial nature of what we actually manage to accomplish. If the ideal level of consideration were not there for purposes of contrast, we would constantly be in danger of ascribing to the parochially proximate a degree of completeness or adequacy to which it has no just claims.

To prohibit our thought from operating at the idealized level that transcends the reach of actual experience would create a profound impoverishment of our intellectual resources. To block off our entry into the sphere of perfection represented by the ideal level of consideration is to cut us off from a domain of thought that characterizes us as intellectually amphibious creatures able to operate in the realm of realities and ideals.

Granted, our expulsion from the Garden of Eden has cut us off from the domain of completeness, perfection, comprehensiveness, and totality. We are constrained to make do with the flawed realities of a mundane and imperfect world. But we aspire to more. Beset by a "divine discontent," we cannot but yearn for that unfettered completeness and perfection, which (as empiricists rightly emphasize) the limited resources of our cognitive situation cannot actually afford us. Not content with graspable satisfactions, we seek far more and press outward "beyond the limits of the possible." It is a characteristic *and worthy* feature of humans to let their thought reach out toward a greater completeness and comprehensiveness than anything actually available within the mundane sphere of secured experience. *Homo sapiens* alone among earthly creatures is a being able and (occasionally) willing to work toward the realization of a condition of things that does not and perhaps even cannot exist—a state of affairs where values are fully and comprehensively embodied. They are agents who can change and transform the world, striving to produce something that does not exist save in the mind's eye, and indeed cannot actually exist at all because its realization calls for a greater perfection and completeness than the recalcitrant conditions of this world allow. Our commitment to this level of deliberation makes us into a creature that is something more than a rational animal—a creature that moves in the sphere of not only ideas but ideals as well.

The Pragmatic Validation of Ideals

What do ideals do for us? What useful role can they play in the human scheme of things? The answer runs something like this: *Homo sapiens* is a rational agent. People can act and must choose among alternative courses of action. This crucial element of choice means that our actions will be guided in the first instance by considerations of "necessity," relating to survival and physical well-being. But to some extent they can, and in an advanced condition of human development *must*, go far beyond this point. Eventually, they come to be guided by necessity-transcending considerations, by man's "higher" aspirations—his yearning for a life that is not only secure and pleasant but also *meaningful*, having some element of excellence or nobility about it. Ideals are the guideposts toward these higher, excellence-oriented aspirations. As such, they motivate rather than constrain, urge rather than demand.

The validation of an ideal is ultimately derivative. It does not lie in the (unrealizable) state of affairs that it contemplates—in that inherently unachievable perfection it envisions. Rather, it lies in the influence that it exerts on the lives of its human exponents through the mediation of thought. To be sure, one ideal can be evaluated in terms of another. But to appraise ideals in a way that avoids begging the question through other idealizations, we do well to leave the domain of idealization altogether and enter into that of the realistically practical. The superiority of one ideal over another must be tested by its *practical consequences* for human well-being. "By their fruits shall ye know them." In appraising ideals we must look not to the *nature* of these ideals alone but also to their *work*. The key role of an ideal is to serve as an instrument of decision making—a sort of navigation instrument for use in the pursuit of the good. And here, the homely practical goods that stand correlative to our needs—survival, health, well-being, human solidarity, happiness, and the like—come into their own once more. Those higher values validate their legitimacy in terms of their bearing on the quotidian ones. The crucial role of ideals lies in their capacity to help us to make the world a better place. There is no conflict between the demands of (valid) practice and the cultivation of (appropriate) ideals. The bearing of the practical and the ideal stand in mutually supportive cooperation.

Such a perspective of course begs the question against the empiricist and sceptic. He wants to play it safe—to have assurances that operations on that empyrean level cannot get us into intellectual or practical mischief. And we must concede to him that such advance assurances cannot be given. We live in a world without guarantees. All we can say is: "Try it, you'll like it—you'll find with the wisdom of hindsight that you have achieved useful results that justify the risks."

The impracticability of its realization is thus no insuperable obstacle to the validation of an ideal. This issue of its feasibility or infeasibility is simply beside the point, because what counts with an ideal is not the question of its attainment but the overall benefits that accrue from its pursuit. Having and pursuing an ideal, regardless of its impracticability, can yield benefits such as a better life for us and a better world for our posterity. The validation of an ideal thus lies in the pragmatic value of its pursuit. As Max Weber observed with characteristic perspicuity, even in the domain of politics, which has been called the art of the possible, "the possible has frequently been attained only through striving for something impossible that lies beyond one's reach."[2]

There are, of course, competing and potentially conflicting ideals. Aldous Huxley wrote:

> About the ideal goal of human effort there exists in our civilization and, for nearly thirty centuries, there has existed a very general agreement. From Isaiah to Karl Marx the prophets have spoken with one voice. In the Golden Age to which they look forward there will be liberty, peace, justice, and brotherly love. "Nation shall no more lift sword against nation"; "the free development of each will lead to the free development of all"; "the world shall be full of the knowledge of the Lord, as the waters cover the sea."[3]

But Susan Stebbing took Huxley sharply to task here:

> In this judgment Mr. Huxley appears to me to be mistaken. There is not now, and there was not in 1937 when Mr. Huxley made this statement, "general agreement" with regard to "the ideal goal of human effort," even in Western Europe, not to mention Eastern Asia. The Fascist ideal has been conceived in sharp-

est opposition to the values which Mr. Huxley believes to be so generally acceptable, and which may be said to be characteristic of the democratic idea. The opposition is an opposition with regard to modes of social organization; it . . . necessitates fundamental differences in the methods employed to achieve aims that are totally opposed. The ideal of Fascism is power and the glorification of the State; the idea of democracy is the development of free and happy human beings; consequently, their most fundamental difference lies in their different conceptions of the worth of human beings as individuals worthy of respect.[4]

And Stebbing is quite right. Potentially conflicting ideals are a fact of life. Different priorities can be assigned to different values, and to prize A over B, is incompatible with prizing B over A. But of course, the prospect of goal alternatives no more invalidates one's ideals than the prospect of spouse alternatives invalidates one's marriage. The justification and power of an ideal inhere in its capacity to energize and motivate human effort toward productive results—in short, in its practical efficacy. Ideals may involve unrealism, but this nowise annihilates their impetus or value precisely because of the practical consequences that ensue upon our adoption of them.

But what are we to make of the fact that competing and conflicting ideals are possible—that not only can different people have different ideals, but one person can hold several ideals that unkind fate can force into situations of conflict and competition ("the devoted spouse" and "the successful politician," for example)?

Clearly, we have to make a good deal of this. Many things follow, including at least the following points: that life is complex and difficult; that perfection is not realizable; that lost causes may claim our allegiance and conflicts of commitment arise; that realism calls on us to harmonize our ideals, even as it requires us to harmonize our other obligations in an overall economy of values. It follows, in sum, that we must make various reciprocal adjustments and compromises. But one thing that does not follow is that ideals are somehow illegitimate and inappropriate.

To attain the limits of the possibilities inherent in our powers and potentialities, we must aim beyond them. And just here lies the great importance of the ideal realm. Human action cannot, in general, be properly understood or adequately managed without a just appreciation of the guiding ideals that lie in the background. For human intervention in the real world sometimes is—and often should be—conditioned by views of the ideal order, in whose direction they find it appropriate to steer the course of events.

This situation has its paradoxical aspect. Ideals may seem to be otherworldly or remote from our practical concerns. But in a wider perspective, they are eminently practical, so that their legitimacy is ultimately pragmatic. The imperative to ideals has that most practical of all justifications in that it enhances the prospects of a more satisfying life. Paradoxical though it may seem, this pragmatic line is the most natural and sensible approach to the validation of ideals.

The general principle of having ideals can be defended along the following lines:

Q: Why should people have ideals at all?

A: Because it is something that is efficient and effective in implementing their pursuit of values.

Q: But why should they care for the pursuit of values?

A: That is simply a part of being human, and thus subject to the fundamental imperative of realizing one's potential of flourishing as the kind of creature one is.

The validity of having ideals inheres in the condition of man as an amphibian, dwelling in a world of both facts and values.

Admittedly, ideals cannot be brought to actualization as such. Their very "idealized" nature prevents the arrangements they envision from constituting part of the actual furnishings of the world. But in the sphere of human endeavor we cannot properly explain and understand the reality about us without reference to motivating ideals. The contemplation of what should ideally be is inevitably bound to play an important role in the rational guidance of our actions.

The validation and legitimation of ideals accordingly lies not in their (infeasible) *applicability* but in their *utility* for directing our efforts—their productive power in providing direction and structure to our evaluative thought and pragmatic action. It is in this, their power to move the minds that move mountains, that the validation and legitimation of appropriate ideals must ultimately reside.

The Grandeur of Ideals

To say that the ultimate legitimation of ideals is pragmatic in orientation is not to say that they are *merely* practical—that they are somehow crass, mundane, and bereft of nobility. By no means! The mode of *justification* of ideals has effectively no bearing on their *nature* at all. Their validation may be utilitarian, but their inherent character remains transcendent. And so there need be nothing crass or mundane about our ideals as such.

With societies and nations, as with individuals, a balanced vision of the good calls for a proportionate recognition of *the domestic impetus* concerned with the well-being of people, home and hearth, stomach and pocketbook, good fellowship, rewarding work, and so on. But it also calls for recognition of *the heroic impetus* concerned with acknowledging ideals, making creative achievements, playing a significant role on the world-historical stage, and doing those splendid things upon which posterity looks with admiration. Above all, this latter impetus involves winning battles, not on the battlefield but in the human mind and spirit. The absence of ideals is bound to impoverish a person or a society. Toward people or nations that have the constituents of material welfare, we may well feel envy, but our *admiration* and *respect* could never be won on this ground alone. Excellence must come into it. And in this excellence-connected domain, we leave issues of utility behind and enter another sphere—that of human ideals relating to man's higher and nobler aspirations.

Homo sapiens is a rational animal. The fact that we are animals squarely places us within the order of nature. But the fact that we are rational exempts us from an absolute rule by external forces. It means that our nature is not wholly *given*, that we are able to contribute in at least some degree toward making ourselves into the sort of creatures we are. A rational creature is inevitably one that has some capacity to let its idealized vision of what it should be determine what it actually is. It is in this sense that an involvement with ideals is an essential aspect of the human condition.

The Practicality of Ideals

Their transcendental and fictional nature accordingly does not destroy the usefulness of ideals. To be sure, we do not—should not—expect to bring our ideals to actual realization. Yet, an ideal is like the Holy Grail of medieval romance: it impels us onward in our journey and gives meaning and direction to our efforts. Rewards of dignity and worth lie in these efforts themselves, irrespective of the question of actual attainment. When appraising a person's life, the question, "What did he endeavor?" is as relevant as the question, "What did he achieve?"

The objects at issue in our ideals are not parts of the world's furniture. Like utopias and mythic heroes (or the real-world heroes we redesign in their image by remaking these people into something that never was), ideals are "larger than life." The states of affairs at issue with ideals do not and cannot exist as such. If we look about us where we will, we shall not find them actualized. The directive impetus that they give us generally goes under the name of "inspiration." They call to us to bend our efforts toward certain unattainable goals. Yet, though fictions, they are eminently *practical* fictions. They find their utility not in application to the things of this world but in their bearing upon the thoughts that govern our actions within it. They are not *things* as such but *thought instrumentalities* that orient and direct our praxis in the direction of realizing a greater good.

Yet ideals, though instruments of thought, are not mere myths. For there is nothing false or fictional about ideals as such—only about the idea of their embodiment in concrete reality. Their pursuit is something that can be perfectly real—and eminently productive. (And it is at this pragmatic level that the legitimation of an ideal must ultimately be sought.)

Still, given the inherent unrealizability of what is at issue, are ideals not indelibly irrational?

Here, as elsewhere, we must reckon with the standard gap between aspiration and attainment. In the practical sphere—for example, in craftsmanship or the cultivation of our health—we may *strive* for perfection, but we cannot ever claim to *attain* it. Moreover, the situation in inquiry is exactly parallel, as is that in morality or in statesmanship. The cognitive ideal of perfected science stands on the same level as the moral ideal of a perfect agent or the political ideal of a perfect state. The value of such unrealizable ideals lies not in the (unavailable) benefits of attainment but in the benefits that accrue from pursuit. The view that it is rational to pursue an aim only if we are in a position to achieve its attainment or approximation is simply mistaken. As we have seen, an unattainable end can be perfectly valid (and entirely rational) if the indirect benefits of its pursuit are sufficient—if in striving after it, we realize relevant advantages to a substantial degree. An unattainable ideal can be enormously productive.

The issue of justifying the adoption of unattainable ideals thus brings us back to the starting point of these deliberations—the defense of the appropriateness of fighting for lost causes. Optimal results are often attainable only by trying for too much—by reaching beyond the limits of the possible. Man is a dual citizen in the realms of reality and possibility. He must live and labor in the one but *toward* the other. The person whose wagon is not hitched to some star or other is not a full-formed human being; he is less than he can and should be.

It seems particularly incongruous to condemn the pursuit of ideals as contrary to *rationality*. For one thing, the crux of rationality lies in the intelligent pursuit of appropriate ends, and ideals constitute a crucial part of the framework, being the points of reference toward which our determinations of appropriateness proceed. No less relevant, however, is the fact that a good case can be made for holding that complete rationality is itself something unrealizable, given the enormously comprehensive nature of what is demanded (for example, by recourse to the principle of total evidence for rationally constituted belief and action). Neither in matters of thought nor in matters of action can we ever succeed in being totally and completely rational; we have to recognize that perfect rationality is itself an unattainable ideal. And we must be realistic about the extent to which we can implement this ideal amid the harsh realities of a difficult world. Yet even though total rationality is unattainable, its pursuit is nevertheless perfectly rational because of the great benefits that it palpably engenders. It is thus ironic that the thoroughgoing rationality, in whose name the adoption of unattainable ends is sometimes condemned, itself represents an unattainable ideal, whose pursuit is rationally defensible only by pragmatically oriented arguments of the general sort considered here.

And so, it is important—and crucially so—for a person to have guiding ideals. A life without ideals need not be a life without purpose, but it will be a life without purposes of a sort in which one can appropriately take reflective satisfaction. The person for whom values matter so little that he or she has no ideals is condemned to wander through life disoriented, without guiding beacons to furnish that sense of direction that gives meaning and a point to the whole enterprise. Someone who lacks ideals suffers an impoverishment of spirit for which no other resources can adequately compensate.[5]

13

Science and Religion

Three points should be clear from the outset:

1. Science does not require God. To answer our scientific questions about the world we need not bring theology into it.

2. Science cannot prove God's existence. We cannot ground theism on scientific facts regarding the observable features of the universe.

3. Scientists are nowadays largely atheists. Many or most of them manage to live successful lives without any religious commitments.

But once these facts are granted we are at the beginning of the story, not at its end. For in the end, the salient question is not whether science involves and requires religious commitment but whether it is compatible—or even congenial—with religion.

Granted, science as such does not require God. (Neither does architecture!) But that of course does not mean that scientists do not need God (or, for that matter, architects). Human life is replete with important issues that do not belong to science. For science is limited by being the very thing it is as a functional enterprise of a certain sort. It is defined by its own characteristic aims and objectives, this being to explain how things work in the world—how recourse to the laws of nature can account for the world's phenomena. But it is (or should be) clear that humans do not live by knowledge alone. There is, of course, more to life than that—more than grasping how nature works. We are creatures not only of understanding but also of doing, not only of thought but of action.

Science and religion have different jobs to do: they are human enterprises with aims and objectives that differ. Science deals with the matter of how things happen in the world—that is, with issues regarding the explanation, prediction, and control of the world's occurrences. Religion, by contrast, addresses normative issues and involves questions of meaning and value—questions bound up with the master question of what we ought to do within our lives and how we ought to conduct them. Regarding the universe that is our home, science takes a *cognitive* approach when asking about the world and its doings. Religion, by contrast, takes an *appreciative* approach of affinity, awe, and wonder. The concern of religion is not from the world as such but from our personal place within it in relation to what is important and meaningful for us. Different enterprises with different goals are at issue: religion cannot do the job of science, nor science that of religion. Overall, both understanding and affectivity have a role in the human scheme of things. And so there is no need for the scientist to scorn religion. For if he is smart he will realize that his lab relates to the work of the inquiring mind, whereas beyond this work of the inquiring intellect there yet remains the work of the appreciative spirit.

Knowledge, after all, is just one component of the constellation of human goods—one valuable project among others, whose cultivation is part of the wider framework of human purposes and interests. Human life is a complicated business, replete with many needs and wants, necessities and possibilities. The prospect of *understanding* and *explaining* the world's ways—of science, in sum—is only one of these. The quality of our lives turns on a broad spectrum of personal and communal desiderata, such as physical well-being, human companionship, environmental congeniality, social harmoniousness, cultural development, spiritual satisfaction, and so on—values and insights that science can often help us attain but which themselves nevertheless fall outside its domain.

The natural scientist deals with the workings of the universe; the fate of particular individuals, be they protozoa or people, does not concern him. But the fate of individuals does concern us—and, in particular, the fate of ourselves as intelligent agents with individual feelings and experiences, needs and morals, opportunities and aspirations. Science is based on generalizations that capture the structural relationship of natural processes. Religion is based on *appreciations* and *inspirations* (revelations included)—on personal experiences that enrich reality and our relationship to it by adding meaning, significance, and value. This "existential" level of our personal life does not concern science, but nevertheless, our religious sentiments can and should paint its enlightening picture. It is not as inquirers but as agents that religion addresses us. Science looks on us—as it looks on all else—as instances of types. The uniqueness of particulars eludes our generality-geared science. And yet that is just exactly what we are: unique particulars. Religion addresses us as individuals. As far as science is concerned, there is nothing special about your parents, your siblings, your children. But the affective dimension of our nature takes a very different line.

An objector may well ask: "But is religious experience and sensibility not itself a proper subject of scientific study?" Of course science can study us humans and submit our thoughts and actions to its objectifying scrutiny. But now the normative dimension of things that is critical to the actual being of a person will be left by the wayside. For observation can report, "People think that X," but of course "People *rightly* think that X" is something else. Again, "People disapprove of Y" can be perfectly appropriate as a scientifically factual report, but "People quite properly disapprove of Y" is something very different. It is one thing to repute and examine experiences and something quite different to have them. (There is little about optics that blind people cannot learn—but they nevertheless miss out on something crucial.) The internalities of reflection and judgments of human existence are something that science does not touch. The affective and spiritual dimension that is critically formative to our status as humans addresses issues that just are not on the scientific agenda.

Psychological science can say: "Those who have a religious or mystical experience claim that it gives them contact with a nature-transcendent sphere of concern." But of course it is only those who actually have this experience that will make such a claim. What people make of their experiences—observational or interpersonal of religions—is up to them—and not up to the external observers who report about it. A crucial difference in "point of view" is at issue in the contact between those who actually experience and those for whom these experiences are mere "phenomena." And so, while science is a crucially important realm of human endeavor, what it will not—and from its own resources cannot—take a position on is this issue of experimental significance and meaning. When science considers religion, it does so *ab extra* and not from within the experiential domain of the believer.

And not only appreciation and evaluation, but also *agency* becomes a crucial factor with respect to religious orientation. Science tells us what we *can* do—can possibly manage to realize—given the talents and resources at our disposal. But it does not and cannot tell us what we *should* do. After all, religion is not a source of factual information about how things stand and work in the world. We will indeed need science to accomplish that job. But there is another job that has to be done: the job of life orientation, of guiding us to a realization of the things that are important, to help us achieve appropriate goals, values, and interests. And here it is religion that seeks to direct our efforts and energies in directions that endow our lives with meaning and rational contentment, to satisfy not just our wants but our deepest needs, to confirm and consolidate the spiritual side of our lives, to encourage us to make the most of choices, and to be able to face the inevitable end of our worldly existence without regret and shame at the loss of opportunities to contribute to the greater good of things.

Pierre-Simon marquis de Laplace was right. To do its own proper explanatory work, science does not need to bring God into it. It is, no doubt, part of scientific wisdom to discount the idea of God as an operative agency—a God of the gaps, whose intervention is invoked to offer a surrogate explanation of the things we do not otherwise understand. Yet, the proper role of faith is not to provide a rational explanation of what happens in the universe, but rather it is to underwrite the idea that such an explanation is always in principle available—something that science cannot quite manage on its own.

Certainly, religion is not, or should not be, viewed as a substitution for science; rather it should—by rights—provide a goad and encouragement to scientific work, motivating the effort to comprehend more fully the nature of God's universe and to avail ourselves of the opportunities that existence upon its stage puts at our disposal.

After all, human agency is in this sense analogous to the divine. When I act within nature—say by moving this piece of paper about— I proceed by natural means. Of course it was I that moved the paper. But I did it by means of hands and arms, of muscles and bone and flesh. To explain *that* the paper moved then and there and *how* the paper moved then and there, you need only refer to physical agencies. Only with the ultimate *why* that reaches outside the course of physical events need you ever make mention of me. But when the questions are about what happens *within* physical nature, the answers are forthcoming in commensurate terms.

"But is a scientist's dedication to knowledge not paramount to a degree where he could only accept a religion whose creedal commitments he would conscientiously consider as truths?" This is doubtless so. But even a conscientious scientist would do well to distinguish between literal and figurative truths, factual and normative truths, informative and orientational truths. After all, the question of what we as individuals should do with our lives and make of the various opportunities at our disposal is not a scientific issue. Once we decide this sort of thing, science can undoubtedly help us to get there. But what our destination should be is a matter not for science but rather for our commitment to goals and values. And this sort of thing is simply outside the province of science, which tells us what the world is like but not what we should do with our lives.

There will, of course, be overlapping issues where both religion and science will enter interactively. Religion calls on us to honor human life by according special treatment to the dead. But science will be needed to decide the question of whether Smith is in fact now dead so that these special procedures are to be instituted. And so, while religion and science are distinct enterprises, they certainly can and should interact with one another.

A further objection may well arise at this point: "Granted, science and religion have different roles to play and different questions to address. But there may well arise some issues in which they come into conflict, such as the age of the universe, the origin of the world, the origin of man, and perhaps others." Now the first thing to note here is that such seeming disagreements are mostly or even generally the products of misunderstandings (as is often the case with disagreements of all sorts). A deeper understanding of just exactly what the religious claims are and a fuller understanding of the scientific issues will often or even generally dissolve the conflict as the product of insufficiently deep understanding, and thereby as more apparent than real. But even were this not the case, there remain various options for coming to terms with such disagreements:

- *Make religion give way to science.* Reconstrue those scientifically problematic religious claims as symbolic, figurative, or metaphorical.

- *Defer judgment.* Realize that scientific understanding is a work in progress that has often changed its mind about things, and thus await with hopefulness a change that will put matters into alignment in the wake of further scientific innovation.

- *Simply combine the two and accept the resulting "inconsistency."* Take the line that we live in a complex, multifaceted world where science is true from its perspective and religion from its, and accept that the two just don't jibe—that different conceptual perspectives can be combined no more than different visual ones can. This in effect leaves their fusion as a mystery that passes our understanding.

- *Take recourse in humility.* Acknowledge that there are many things we just don't understand and that reconciling present, seeming divergences between science and religion may just be one of them. (After all, who knows how hypnotism or acupuncture work?)

Clearly, the "conflict between science and religion" does not leave one without options. So, a religion between can hold to the idea that in cases of conflict some sort of reconsideration will in the end prove possible.

But now consider the objection: "I want to be a modern, scientific person, who bases belief on the teachings of science. And science does not speak for religion: one cannot base theism on scientific facts." Well, so be it. But the reality of it is that we stand committed to lots of things that we cannot base on scientific facts. Are the challenges and rewards of living based on science? We do—or should—have a special care for and about our parents, brothers, spouses. Does science establish them as more lovable and worthy of our affection than other people? We try to earn the respect of others. Does science teach us that respect for others—or self-respect for that matter—is a paramount value? Do we base our values on the teachings of science rather than the impetus of our natural human feelings? It is simply not through science that we configure out loyalties, our allegiances, our values. Science tells us about *facts*; but their significance—religious significance included—will and must come from somewhere else. And it is just here that religious commitment comes into it.

With regard to the question of the existence of God, the great mathematician-astronomer Laplace offered the remark, "I had no need for that hypothesis." And this is certainly correct. For scientific questions have to be based on scientific principles. With respect to how things work in the cosmos, the authority of science will be complete. If we want to know *how it is* that there are microbes in the world, we had best turn to biological science. But there are also questions that lie above and beyond the voice of science. And the question of *why it is* that the world is such that there are microbes in it is one of these. For what is basically at stake here is a value issue, presumably to the general effect that a world with microbes in it has some significant advantage over alternatives. Of course someone might say that such a question is improper and illegitimate—that if an issue makes sense at all then science can resolve it. But this decidedly radical stance of scientism (as it is usually called) is a matter not of good sense but of a rather radical and decidedly problematic ideology.

Science-inspired antireligionists often support their position by portraying theism as merely the response to a psychological need. Their reasoning goes essentially like this: "Humans are weak and vulnerable creatures existing in a difficult and often seemingly hostile world. As such, they have a mere psychological need for reassurance that the world is a user-friendly habitat functioning under the auspices of a benign creative agent or agency." Now, to speak of something as "a *mere* psychological need of man" draws close to self-contradiction. There is nothing "mere" about such needs. When a psychological need achieves generality it thereby achieves a sort of objective validity as well. Given the realities of human development, it is bound to reflect something that has survived in the operations of a rational creature, thereby betokening an efficacy that serves to evidentiate objective validity. Even as our felt need for food would not be there if our bodies were not sustained by nourishment, so our felt need for spiritual sustenance could not be there if the world's spiritual forces did not sustain it. But there is also another problem about consigning religions to the limbo of a "mere psychological need." For this argument effectively shoots itself in its own foot. Unbelievers who deploy it are using a weapon that can just as readily be deployed against them. "Humans are willful and arrogant beings to whom the thought of an all-observing and stern judge who condemns their wicked ways is intimidating and daunting. And accordingly, they have a psychological need to be liberated from this prospect. Their unbelief is no more than a response to a psychological need." The upshot is clear: the argument from psychological need is a two-edged sword that cuts both ways—alike against theism and atheism. Argumentation from need is a wash.

"But where is the evidence that speaks for the truth of religion?" This question has to be approached from the opposite end—from the angle of the question, "If those religious contentions were indeed true, what sort of evidence for this fact could we reasonably expect to obtain for it?" After all, belief in God is the sort of thing that is not a matter of scientific observation and theory. We do not, cannot, and should not expect astronauts to come back with reports of angelic encounters in outer space. (As Nikita Khrushchev once complained, they did not.) It has to be through inner urgings and the impetus of our hearts that people are led to religion, not through outer observation. So, if there were indeed a benevolent God, we would expect that at least in the long run (and not necessarily the short) and at least in the aggregate (and not necessarily everywhere) that those who live lives mindful of God's suppositions would derive some benefit thereby. And if it is miracles we demand, then is not our very life itself a constant reminder of the miracles in nature? Is not this sort of evidence the best and most one could reasonably expect?

What is it you want? Tablets from the mountain? Voices from the clouds? Been there, done that; you just missed it, sorry. The best available evidence for physical theories is experimentation in the physical laboratory; the best available evidence for medical drugs is by clinical trials; the best available evidence for religion is by experimentation and trials in the laboratory of life. Are nonbelievers happier, better, more contented people than believers? Or is it the other way round? Look about and see for yourself. Here as elsewhere we must allow the indications of the evidence to speak.

The reality of it is that science itself is not exempt from "faith in things unseen." Nothing guarantees that the phenomena are always and everywhere as they are within our range of observation. Nothing guarantees that the laws and regularities that have been in operation in cosmic history will continue unchanged in the future. Nothing guarantees that other universes (if such there are—and we presumably cannot get there from here) have any even remote resemblance of ours. That nature's laws are as we think them to be is something we cannot know for sure, but can only hope.

To be sure, the hope that underpins the inductive proceedings of science is geared to the objectives of the enterprise—to expecting enhanced *cognitive* returns. And it is not for the sake of enhanced knowledge of world explanative facts that we turn to religion. But is not the source of the grandeur of scientific hopefulness equaled by that of religion in relation to the distinctive character of this particular enterprise as a means to situating oneself meaningfully within a difficult and complex world?

"But surely scientists are among the smartest people there are, and for the most part they are not religious." This objection, too, is inappropriate. For one thing, religiosity just is not a matter of smarts—of calculation, of figuring things out by brain power! It is, rather, a matter of having a reflective perspective on matters of life, death, and man's place in reality's great scheme of things—of having a certain stance toward the world we live in and in which reactions like awe and wonder are significant and responses like worshipful humility figure significantly.

The idea that it is inappropriate for a scientist to be religious because the majority of scientists are not theists is quite misguided. After all, scientists themselves do not proceed in this manner. It is not part of the scientific mentality to "go with the flow" and accept what the majority thinks. Scientists try to figure things out for themselves as best they can.

Moreover, the reality of it is that while the majority of scientists are (probably) atheists, a very sizable minority are theists of one sort or another. Certainly this has been so traditionally from Galileo to Newton to Maxwell to Einstein. But even today many fine scientists are theists, and in some fields—cosmological physics in particular—they often even put their theism in touch with their scientific work.

"But the idea of an intelligent creator just doesn't make sense. After all, the universe has developed by some sort of cosmic evolution. And any sort of evolutionary product is inefficient, slow, and wasteful. Surely an intelligent creator would do better." This sort of objection is predicated on the idea that an intelligent creator would not opt for getting physical reality under way by a process of cosmic evolution proceeding developmentally from some un-state inaugurated in a big bang-like initiation event. The objector seems to think it would only be fitting to the divine dignity to inaugurate a universe by zapping it into existence in medias res, as a development-dispensing concern. It is, however, not readily apparent why this would be preferable. And it poses some distinctive problems of its own—for example, why the universe should not have been created five minutes ago completely fitted out with geological traces, human memories, and so on.

As noted before, it would be a profound error to oppose evolution to intelligent design—to see these two as somehow conflicting and incompatible. For natural selection—the survival of forms better able to realize self-replication in the face of challenges and overcome the difficulties posed by the world's vicissitudes—affords an effective means to intelligent resolutions.

"But in the light of such utilitarian considerations religion is perhaps simply a matter of the evolution-engendered impetus to believe, leaving truth altogether by the wayside, and thereby bereft of rational legitimacy." Yet would this conclusion really follow? Is conceding that a certain instinct has evolution's "Good Housekeeping Seal of Approval" not already to concede to it a solid basis in fact? To say that religious belief is "no more" than the product of an evolutionary instinct is to have a strange idea about what can be considered "no more." Indeed, to say that a belief instinct is founded in evolution is automatically to concede to it a significant evidential basis in the world's operative realities. Evolution is not a process that favors the misguided, deceitful, and false.

As Darwin himself already noted in his *Descent of Man*, "belief in all-pervading spiritual agencies seems to be universal." And on the basis of evolutionary principles it is difficult to imagine that this would be so if such a belief were not somehow survival conducive. Clearly, belief in an ultimately benign cosmos is likely to benefit agents of finite intelligence who must constantly act in the expectation that things will turn out well. And this is going to require the suitable backing of fact. Are not things that taste good generally edible and things that taste bad not generally harmful? Is not the tendency to believe that things are as our experience indicates them to be generally correct as well as essential to the conduct of life? Does evolution itself not proceed via a systemic coordination of utility and correctness? Evolutionary grounding surely constitutes a positive credential rather than a refutation. After all, evolution will not back losers. For belief-motivated agents, cognitive adequacy is bound to be survival conducive. Evolution will not—cannot—imprint us with tendencies that are systematically counterproductive—even optical illusions take root in processes that work to our advantage. Its motto is: survival of the most advantageous. And which is more advantageous for us: truth or falsehood? Will it be advantageous for us to think that hostiles are friends and friends unfriendly, that poisons nourish and nourishments poison, that small objects are large and large ones small? There may be forces at work in the universe that engender tendencies to systematic error, but evolution is not one of them.

"But what of the untold suffering that has been—and is—imposed on mankind in the name of religion?" All one can say here is that condemnation by association is not sensible—any more than guilt by association is. Pretty much anything useful in human affairs has the potential of abuse as well. The knife that helps to feed us can murder as well. The medicine that can cure can also poison. The police that sustain our peace can be an instrument of oppression. The religions that should by rights sustain brotherhood can make for enmity. All this is true and regrettable. But there is nothing unique or different here—we confront a fact of life that prevails throughout the realm of human affairs. If we refrain from resorting to those things that admit of abuse, then there is little we would be able to accomplish in this life.

Moreover, people in glass houses should not throw stones. When complaining of harm done in the name of religion, one should not entirely overlook harm done under the auspices of science. Those greatest of all physics experiments, atomic bombs, have killed far more people than were ever lynched. The medical experimentation of the Nazi extermination camps killed more people than the Spanish Inquisition. The complex machinery of informed consent in matters of pharmacology and medicine represent so many ventures in closing barn doors after fled horses.

"But what of all the wicked and even crazy things that people have done—and are doing—in the name of religion?" Here again condemnation by association does not work. Because some people pursue a project in evil ways does not mean that everyone need do so. The situation is akin to the injunction, "Find yourself a profession." Clearly, the existence of wickedness in the group should not deter one from being a doctor, baker, or candlestick maker. One need not be estranged from religion by the fact that some practitioners are nasty any more than an accountant or professor need be. And of course the same thing goes for scientists as well. The proverbial "mad scientist" does not annihilate the value of the whole venture. To reject being affiliated to the wicked is to resign from the human race.

"But so far it has only been argued that a scientifically-minded person can be religious: that various obstacles and objections can be removed. But it is one thing to hold that something can be done, and something else to hold that it should be done. So why should a modern scientifically-minded person adopt a religion?" The answer is that one should only do so if one wants to: only if there is urging in one's inner nature that impels one in this direction. But of course, human nature being what it is, this is something that is likely to be the case—at least potentially—with all of us. For when we consider our place in the world's vast scheme of things, all of us are liable to that sense of awe and wonder that lies at the basis of religiosity and to yearn for a reassurance of our worth and dignity that only faith (and not knowledge) can provide for us. Man—*Homo sapiens*—is a rational animal. And what lifts us above the level of animality is the process through which we come to knowledge—and preeminently scientific knowledge, which includes us regarding the limits and limitations that call for a confirmation of meaning and value to which religious faith alone can adequately respond.

"But can't I lead an ethically good and evaluatively fruitful life without religion?" Certainly you can! Many people manage to do so. But it's a bit harder. It's like asking, "Can't I be a good violin player without lots of practice?" or "Can't I be a fluent Mandarin speaker if I only start learning at thirty?" It can be done. Some very fortunate people can pull it off. But it is not easy—and scarcely practicable for most of us.

"But all these considerations are vague and directionally inconclusive. They speak for having a religion but do not resolve the issue of which one." True enough. So what is one to make of the plurality of religions? The reality of different religions is a fact of life. Throughout the history of human civilization, different forms of religious commitment have coexisted on our planet. And it is perfectly clear why this should be so. For religions at once reflect and actualize how people relate to transcendent or "ultimate" realities that create and shape the world we live in and our destiny within it. But of course here, as elsewhere, how people relate to things is determined by their issue-relevant experience. And since people differently situated in variant historical and cultural contexts have different courses of experience, there are bound to be different religions. After all, some religions are simply unavailable to people for historical reasons. The ancient Greeks of Homer's day could not have become Muslims or Christians. And cultural context will clearly be another limiting factor. Some religions are inaccessible to people because the whole issue of their experience points them in altogether different directions. The Englishmen of the era of Pusey and Newman could be Nonconformist or Anglican—or Roman Catholic. They could not really have joined the Shinto faith, let alone that of the Mayans or the Aztecs. Cultural contexts limit the range of available options. And for particular individuals even one's personal and idiosyncratic temperament will limit the alternatives that are realistically available to people. So it seems as though the issue of religious pluralism is going to have to be personalistically relativized. There being many religions, the question—seemingly—will be, "Which one of these various possibilities is going to be right for me—or for X?" For the individual, there is going to be a limit to the range of possibilities, what William James characterized as "live options." In his characteristically vivid prose he wrote:

> Ought it, indeed, to be assumed that the lives of all men should show identical religious elements? In other words, is the existence of so many religious types and sects and creeds regrettable? To these questions I answer "No" emphatically. And my reason is that I do not see how it is possible that creatures in such different positions and with such different powers as human individuals are, should have exactly the same functions and the same duties. No two of us have identical difficulties, nor should we be expected to work out identical solutions. Each, from his peculiar angle of observation, takes in a certain sphere of fact and trouble, which each must deal with in a unique manner . . . If an Emerson were forced to be a Wesley, or a Moody forced to be a Whitman, the total human consciousness of the divine would suffer.[1]

So, while there indeed are various religions, the reality of it is that the range of religions that are realistically available to a given individual is drastically curtailed. In adopting a religion, as in adopting a profession or selecting a place to live, you have to make up your own mind on the basis of the best information you have the time and energy to collect. And the range is confined by potent constraints and depends upon the person's culture, environment, familial situation, personal disposition, and the like, to an extent that often as not narrows the range of alternatives down to one. The question, "What religion is right for me?" is for most of us analogous to that of choosing a language. One's cultural context does the job for most of us. Of course there is some modest degree of choice—we can with great effort tear ourselves loose to go elsewhere. But only if you do so as a small child will the result ever be completely natural. The individual who shifts to another language as an adult will never speak it entirely as a native. And those who are able to make even a halfway successful job of it are comparatively few and far between.

"But is not this sort of position that of an indifferentist relativism ('it's all just a matter of taste and inclination—there is no rhyme or reason to it.')?" No, it certainly is not. Rather, it is that of a reasoned contextualism based on what is appropriate for people given the circumstances of their particular situation. And contexts can grow—especially under the impetus of expanding experience, personal and vicarious. And there is, of course, no reason why these circumstances should not include a critical scrutiny of the alternatives. For religions are not created equal. An intelligent and enterprising person should not hesitate to explore the options: a religion is not a gift horse into whose mouth one should not look critically.

But what sense can one make of the question, "Is there one single, uniquely best and appropriate religion?" What sort of cogent case could the antipluralist advocate of "one uniquely true religion" possibly have in view?

To all visible intents and purposes this question comes down to: "Is there one religion which any rational person would accept given the opportunity—that is, would freely choose in the light of full information about it and its alternatives?" We are, to all appearance, driven back to Kant's question about "religion within the limits of reason alone."

On this basis someone could well protest: "Does not this very approach seriously prejudice matters by prejudging a very fundamental issue? For does it not put reason in the driver's seat by putting it in the role of the arbiter of religion? And does it thus not ride roughshod over Pascal's insistence that some human fundamentals are properly matters of the mind and others of the heart?"

But this objection simply has to be put aside as contextually inappropriate. If that question about the one true and optimal religion is indeed meaningful, then there will and must be a pre-commitment neutral, rationally cogent answer to it that is being demanded. We have no sensible alternative here. What sort of answer to our question could we want that is not reasonable? For sure, it would make no sense to assess the merit of religions on their own telling. Some commitment-neutral standpoint is needed. And what better place is there to go than the realm of reason?

So, what is it that our rationality has to say on the matter? If it is our intent and purpose to proceed objectively and appraise religions on a basis that involves no prior substantive religious commitments, then we have no real alternative but to proceed functionally—to go back to square one and begin with the question of the aims and purposes that religions serve as modes of human belief and practice. And so there is really only one path before us. It is—prepare for a shock!—the way of pragmatism, that is, of a functionally oriented inquiry into the question of what religion optimally accomplishes, the aims and purposes for which religions are instituted as operative practices within human communities. For if what lies before us is the question of religious optimality—of which of those multiple religions is to qualify as best—then the question of "How for the best?" simply cannot be avoided. At this stage, we have no realistic alternative but to view religions in a purposive light and inquire into the aims and purposes of the enterprise, asking: "Why is it that people should undertake a religious commitment at all? What sensible human purpose is realized by making a religious commitment a significant part of one's life? What's in it for us—to put it crassly?" In approaching religion from such a practicalist point of view—inquiring into the human aims and objectives that adherence to a religion can and should facilitate—one is going to come up with a list such as this:

- Providing a framework for understanding the world and our personal place within it that energizes what Abraham Lincoln called, "the better angels of our nature."
- Providing a focus for the sense of awe, wonder, and worship as we puny creatures confront a natural world of vast extent and

power, giving a sense of comfort in the face of the vast forces beyond our control. And possibilizing powerful interaction with the agency that governs the fate of all they hold dear.

- Providing an evaluative appreciation of the universe and giving an impetus to human productivity and creativity within it. Enabling a frail and vulnerable creature to feel "at home" in the universe and strengthening the sense of opportunity to have a "meaningful life."

- Providing people with a perspective that gives their lives a meaningful position in the universe's grand scheme of things, providing them a worldview supportive of human aspirations and diminishing any sense of futility, alienation, and dehumanization.

- Providing a sense of social solidarity with our fellows and an appreciation of the worth and dignity of human potential in a way that strengthens the fabric of mutual concern, care, and respect for one another, resulting in a diminishing of man's inhumanity to man.

Then too, there is the role of religion in easing people's anguish and anxiety in the face of life's frustrations and difficulties. The spiritual impact of "lifting people's spirits" is a vibrant reality. In augmenting the quality of their lives and enhancing their performance in meeting life's challenges, religion can and should make a positive contribution to the quality of life.

On this basis, it emerges that a complex fabric of potential psychological, social, and cognitive benefits are at issue with a person's commitment to a religion. In other words, there is—or can be— something in it for us. And a chain of natural connections links all of these by a line that runs from cosmic congeniality to individual self-worth, to the worth of our peers, to human solidarity at large. More than any other ideological posture, religious faith makes manifest "the power of positive thinking." Without religion, in sum, it is somewhere between difficult and impossible to realize various salient positivities that are conducive, and perhaps even to some extent indispensable, to human flourishing.

We confront the question of compassion, where to all appearances the best we can then do is to apply the standard of humanity itself and ask: "What form of religion most effectively succeeds in calling forth the best in people and most supportively energizes them into a way of life that deserves our admiration and respect?" Within the narrow confines that are now upon us, this seems to be the best and most one can do to affect an "objective" comparison. For without serious commitment to the cultivation of the great goods, whose pursuit is an opportunity afforded us by human existence—goodness, happiness, virtue, beauty, knowledge—a religion builds on sandy ground. Even without question-begging precommitments, we can look at religions not only subjectively, in terms of their capacity to speak to us personally, but more impersonally, in terms of their capacity to address larger issues that confront all of us relative to the challenges of creating an intellectually and emotionally satisfying life within the circumstances of a complex and often difficult world. Where entry into a community of faith is concerned, we humans, as rational beings, are not just entitled but effectively obligated to look for a religion that is intellectually satisfying, personally congenial, and socially benign. A religion whose theologians avoid the difficult questions, whose preachers do not engage the sympathy of our hearts, and whose practitioners are not energized to exert effort for the general good of mankind and the alleviation of suffering is surely thereby one unworthy of enlisting the allegiance of sensible and sensitive people.

Admittedly, there is little doubt that, judged by the aforementioned standards, the record of all of the world's major religions is rather spotty. Unquestionably, our religions—like all other human enterprises and mutilations—will reflect the frailties and imperfections of our species by the fact of its being a structure built up of and by what Kant called the crocked timber of humanity. But the issue is not one of perfection. It is a matter of the seriousness of effort and the comparative extent of success.

To be sure, someone who becomes religious only from considerations of "What's in it for me" is not an authentically religious person at all. But the crux is that religious commitment is *transformative*. No matter how you enter—even if for reasons of human solidarity, let alone for crass and self-advantaging motives—you will not manage to remain there. Commitment, no matter how modest at first, will undergo a natural process of growth.[2]

14

On the Improvability of the World

The Improvability Thesis

Since Voltaire, most people have thought it absurd of Leibniz to deem this vale of tears to be the best of possible worlds. And what principally gives people pause here is that they see this world as imperfect on grounds of potential remediation. Laplace, for one, maintained that, given the chance, he could readily improve on the natural world's arrangements. And other bold spirits often think the same. It is perfectly clear, so they say, that this, that, or the other modification would make this a better world. And from there it is only one short and easy step to the conclusion that a benevolent creator does not exist.[1]

All the same, this idea that the world is improvable by tinkering is deeply problematic. The task of the discussion is to show how this is so.

Non-Improvability vs. Theory and Optimalism

The idea that the actual world as we have it is the best possible goes back to Plato's *Timaeus*:

The divine being (*theos*) wished that everything should be good and nothing imperfect AS FAR AS POSSIBLE (*kata dunamin*) . . . since he judged that order (*taxis*) was better than disorder. For him who is the supremely good, it neither was nor is permissible to do anything other than what is the best [among the possibilities].[2]

What Plato envisions is a world that, imperfections notwithstanding, will nevertheless be optimal—that is, "for the best"—in being just as perfect as the realities of the situation permit.

From Leibniz onward, the optimalist has faced the charge of being a Dr. Pangloss who will acknowledge no evil in the world—much like that familiar trio of wise monkeys who "see no evil, hear no evil, speak no evil." So what is it that could possibly favorably incline someone to Leibniz's contention that this is the best of possible worlds?

Well, there is, to begin with, the consideration, to which none of us can be wholly indifferent, that this is the world in which we ourselves exist. One can hardly avoid seeing this circumstance in a favorable light. Dr. Seuss captures the point admirably:

> [W]orse than all that . . . Why, you might be a WASN'T!
> A Wasn't has no fun at all. No it doesn't.
> A Wasn't just isn't. He just isn't present.
> But you . . . You ARE YOU! And now isn't that pleasant![3]

Then, there is also the more impersonal consideration that this is a world whose developmental processes have brought intelligent beings into existence. This too one cannot but see as a good thing.

To be sure, such considerations merely argue for *good* and not yet for *best*. This is something that has to be based on more complex considerations.

What most fundamentally stands in the way of conjectural improvability is the pervasive interconnectedness of things. This means there is no real prospect of local tinkering with the world without wider ramifications. In this world—and indeed in any possible world—states of affairs are so interconnected that local changes always have pervasive consequences.

The domain of fact has a systemic integrity that one disturbs at one's own peril: a change at any point has reverberations everywhere. Once you embark on a reality-modifying assumption, then as far as pure logic is concerned all bets are off. Any local "fix" always has involvements throughout, and consequently, no tweaking or tinkering may be able to effect an improvement. For the introduction of belief-contravening hypotheses puts everything at risk. In their wake, nothing is safe anymore. To maintain consistency, you must revamp the entire fabric of fact, which is to say that you confront a task of Sisyphean proportions. (This is something that those who make glib use of the idea of other possible worlds all too easily forget.) Reality is something too complex to be remade anymore than fragmentally by our thought, which can effectively come to terms only with piecemeal changes *in* reality but not with comprehensive changes *of* reality. Reality's reach has a grip that it will never entirely relax: it is a tightly woven web where the cutting of any thread leads to an unraveling of the whole.

The fact is that limitedness is inevitable with finite beings. Humans cannot be superhuman. But imperfections of various sorts accompany any class of items, so that a world cannot be devoid of imperfections. If you want animals, you must provide them with organic food. And a food chain brings with it a nature rough in tooth and claw. All worldly arrangements have a downside that involves imperfection.

But all the same, imperfection does not preclude optimality. All that is required here is that—notwithstanding whatever imperfections there are and whatever positivities there might be—no other possible world arrangement ranks higher overall. An imperfect world is not thereby automatically improvable. For the reality of it is that improvement faces major obstacles.

The Butterfly Effect as a Substantive Obstacle to Optimalism

"But how can you claim that the world is all that meritorious and benignly designed? Surely, envisioning a better world would not be all that hard. After all, it wouldn't have taken much to arrange some small accident that would have removed a Hitler or a Stalin from the scene. To figure out how this sort of thing could be arranged—to the world's vast improvement—is not rocket science!"

Alas, dear objector, even rocket science is not good enough. For what stands in the way here is the massive obstacle of what is known as the butterfly effect. This phenomenon takes root in the *sensitive dependence of outcomes on initial conditions* in chaos theory, where a tiny variation in the initial conditions of a dynamic system can issue immense variations in the long term behavior of the system. E. N. Lorenz first analyzed the effect in a pioneering 1963 paper, which caused a meteorologist to remark that "if the theory were correct, one flap of a sea gull's wings would be enough to alter the course of the weather forever."[4] With this process, changing even one tiny aspect of nature—one single flutter of a butterfly's wings—could have the most massive repercussions: tsunamis, droughts, ice ages, there is no limit. With this phenomenology in play, rewriting the course of the cosmos in the wake of even the smallest hypothetic change is an utter impracticability.

A *chaotic condition*, as natural scientists nowadays use this term, obtains when we have a situation that is tenable or viable in certain circumstances but where a change in these circumstances—even one that is extremely minute—will destabilize the overall situation with imponderable consequences, producing results that cannot be foreseen in informative detail. Any hypothetical change in the physical makeup of such a world—however small—sets in motion a vast cascade of further such changes, either in regard to the world's furnishings or in the laws of nature.

For all we can tell, reality is just like that. And now suppose that we make only a very small alteration in the descriptive composition of the real, say by adding one pebble to the river bank. But which pebble? Where are we to get it, and what are we to put in its place? And where are we to put the air or the water that this new pebble displaces? Moreover, the region within six inches of the new pebble used to hold N pebbles. It now holds $N + 1$. Of which region are we to say that it holds $N - 1$. If it is that region yonder, then how did the pebble get here from there? By a miraculous instantaneous transport? By a little boy picking it up and throwing it, but then, which little boy? And how did he get there? And if he threw it, then what happened to the air that his throw displaced that would otherwise have gone undisturbed? Here problems arise without end.

As we conjure with those pebbles, what about the structure of the envisioning electromagnetic, thermal, and gravitational fields? Just how are these to be preserved, as was given in the removal and/or shift of the pebbles above? How is matter to be readjusted to preserve consistency here? Or are we to do so by changing the fundamental laws of physics?

What the butterfly effect means is that we can no longer be glibly facile about our ability to tinker with reality to effect improvements in the world by somehow removing this or that among its patent imperfections through well-intentioned readjustments. For what would need to be shown is that such a repair would not yield unintended, and indeed altogether unforeseen, consequences resulting in an overall inferior result. And this would be no easy task—and indeed could prove to be one far beyond our feeble powers.

"But could this situation not have been avoided altogether? After all, that butterfly effect is the result of the fact that, in certain respects, the laws of nature have yielded a system of the sort that mathematicians characterize as chaotic. Surely one could change the laws of nature to avoid this result." It is no doubt so. But now we have leapt from the frying pan into the fire. For in taking this line we propose to fiddle not merely with this or that specific occurrence in world history, but are engaged in conjuring with the very laws of nature themselves. And this embarks us on the uncharted waters of a monumental second-order butterfly effect—one whose implications and ramifications are incalculable. The point is simple: Yes, the world's particular existing negativities are indeed remediable in theory. But to avert them in practice would require accepting an even larger array of negativities overall. The cost of avoiding those manifest evils of this world would then be the realization of an even larger mass of misfortune.

But is it actually the case—really and truly—that the imperfect arrangements of this world nevertheless leave it in the position of overall optimality? It would certainly take an intelligence far more powerful than mine—and perhaps even than *ours*—to establish so difficult and contentious a claim, something that would require surveying in distributive detail an effectively unsurveyable manifold of items. It would clearly be an act of hubris to assert categorically one's ability to demonstrate that the world as we have it cannot possibly be improved upon when everything is taken into account. But the very fact that the doorway of possibility is open here shows that the violation of common sense objection cannot be sustained. For here, as so often elsewhere, common sense must in the final analysis be prepared to yield to deeper considerations.

The Package Deal Predicament

The world we have—and indeed any possible alternative to it—is a package deal. Once we start tinkering with it, it seeps through our fingers like water. In seeking to change it, we create conditions where there is no longer any anaphoric "it" to deal with. To tinker with a world is to abolish it—to replace it by something else.

And this something else could readily prove to be worse overall. To render this idea graphic, one should consider W. W. Jacobs' chilling story of *The Monkey's Paw*, whose protagonist is miraculously granted wishes that actually come true—but always at a fearful price. Granted, the world's *particular*, existing negativities are indeed remediable in theory, but to arrange for this will likely entail an even larger array of negativities overall (The Monkey's Paw effect). The cost of avoiding those manifest evils of this world would then be the realization of an even larger mass of misfortune. The thesis here is effectively that of Leibniz: it is not intended to claim that the world is *perfect*, but just that it is *optimal*—the best possible with the emphasis not on *best* but on *possible*.

The upshot of these considerations is thus clear. The idea that the world's defects can be fixed by tinkering is decidedly implausible. And given the fact that rendering the world as a whole lies beyond our feeble powers, we have to face up to the consideration that—for all we can tell—this is indeed the best of possible worlds, and that changing the existing condition of the universe in any way whatsoever will diminish the sum total of its positivities. We have to face the prospect that there is no "quick fix" for the negativities of this world.

The reality of it is that merit maximization at the global level viewed collectively, neither entails nor requires merit maximization at the local level viewed distributively. The world's constituent components are certainly not as perfect as can be. It is perfectly possible that they are interconnected (via the butterfly effect) in such a way that improving one substantial element or aspect can be achieved only at a dispositionally higher cost in terms of merit diminution elsewhere. As concerns merit, the existing situation could well be the best overall arrangement of things—its manifest defects to the contrary notwithstanding.

For the sake of a (certainly crude) illustration of the sort of situation at issue, consider the hypothetical microworld subject to the following requirement:

> Let A represent a factor of positive merit. Let X be an environmental condition relevant to A's existence, subject to the idea that an A can only be sustained in being when three X's are laterally adjacent. And finally, let it be that the "space" of our world consists of a 4 x 4 rectangular grid.

In these circumstances, the optimal arrangement of affairs can only take the form:

	X	A	X
X	A	X	A
A	X	A	X
X	A	X	

Or any of its variants by 90° rotation. Now, to be sure, matters can indeed be improved upon locally—any one of these X-occupied positions could in theory accommodate an A. But globally, matters could not be improved upon. Any attempt to replace an X by an A would impel matters into an inferior result overall.

World optimization is always maximization under various existential constraints imposed by the types of things whose realization is being contemplated. And such constraints mean that while the world may well be as good as it can be *as a whole*—that is, is aggregatively merit maximizing—nevertheless, it is not correspondingly merit maximizing in its parts taken distributively. The condition of many of these parts is far from optimal and can certainly be improved. It is just that the merit of the parts is so interconnected and intertwined that improvement in one area is bound to carry with it diminution in another.

We shall characterize as a teeter-totter condition any arrangement where an improvement in regard to one aspect can only be achieved at the cost of worsening matters in another respect. Whenever this situation is in play, it stands decisively in the way of absolute perfection, and this line of thought vividly indicates how "fixing" local imperfections can readily fail to tell against global optimality.

The Problem of Evil or the Dr. Pangloss Objection of World Improvability

Yet what is one to make of such an optimalism?

Note, to begin with, that the idea that this is the best of *possible* worlds is not an occasion for unmixed delight and unalloyed rejoicing. For to characterize the world as the best possible is not necessarily optimism but is perfectly compatible with the decidedly pessimistic lament that, notwithstanding the many manifest imperfections of this world, the sad fact remains that all of the alternatives available in the manifold of possibility are yet worse.

So, the world cannot be *perfect*. But why should it not be *better*? As acknowledged earlier, the optimalist has inherited a Leibnizian problem, facing the charge of being a Dr. Pangloss who will acknowledge no evil in the world.

The traditional line of response to this sort of objection has two parts that respectively pivot on the distinction between moral and physical evil—between misfortunes that originate through the deliberate agency of intelligent beings, and those that, like earthquakes, storms, and other natural disasters, originate through the impersonal operations of nature.

The traditional explanation of *natural* evils looks to several distinct ways of addressing the problem of the world's misfortunes and suffering:

- To dismiss natural evil as mere illusion, as only apparent but not real. This is the illusionism of Oriental mysticism and of the Panglossian unrealism that Voltaire mistakenly attributed to Leibniz.

- To see it as part of the indispensable causal means to a greater good. (The melodrama must have its villain so that the threatened maiden can fully appreciate the delights of a heroic rescue.)

- To see it as (noncausally) compensated for in the larger scheme of things—that is, either in this world or the next. (This, according to Kant, is the rationale for belief in an afterlife.)
- To see it as the collateral damage that is unavoidable in even the best of possible arrangements contrived with a view to the realization of certain, salient positivities.

For the sake of brevity, these four approaches might be designated as the theories of *illusion, mediation, compensation,* and *necessitation.* The optimalistic approach adopts the last of these options, taking the line that natural evil represents the price of an entry ticket into the best possible arrangements within the limits of certain constraints. Physical and moral evils, in sum, are seen as the inescapable consequences that are bound to occur when beings of limited capacity come to be emplaced within a world order, whose lawfulness is, on the one hand, a requisite for their existence but, on the other hand, leads unavoidably to circumstances disfavorable to the interest and well-being of some.

A world—a viable world setting for intelligent agents—must have a manifold of laws to provide order in the unfolding of its phenomena. But in and of themselves, laws and rules will not always produce the best conceivable results. The player with the best technique may not win, and the artist who adheres to all the appropriate rules may not produce the best result. Perhaps the best process will indeed often or usually or morally produce the best product—but by no means always and markedly. Optimality of process is compatible with suboptimality of product.

Admittedly, one would not think all that well of a world with splendid processes but terrible occurrences. But where a sensible optimalism is concerned, the contrast between process and product is softened by the consideration that the best process is that which is most apt for and most favorable to the generation of optimal principles. The point is that holistic optimality is a complex idea in which *both* process- *and* occurrence-optimality will play a cooperatively (partially) determent role. Whenever these two desiderata diverge significantly, some sort of intermediate compromise will have to be worked out in the interest of a meaningful overall result.

And so, the presently envisioned optimalism geared to the interests of intelligent beings will gear itself specifically to those laws that augur good results for intelligent beings. That "best possible" world at issue is accordingly one that procedural arrangements are such as to optimize (and indeed maximize) the *chances* of a good result. But nevertheless, it will not—cannot—guarantee this outcome. It may (and doubtless will) set the stage in the way most favorable to good outcomes for intelligent beings, but nevertheless these finite creatures, being limited alike in knowledge, power, and good will, will all too often encounter misfortunes in the natural course of world history.

On the other hand, the traditional explanation of *moral* evil attributes this to the consequences of free will, it being inevitable that creatures of limited intelligence and endowed with free choice not only can but will act for wrong as well as right, evil as well as good. Moral evil is thus seen as the unavoidable price to be paid for a world whose agents combine finite capabilities with freedom of choice.

To be sure, this line of argument, often cited as the free will defense of a world with moral evil, has evoked the objection: "Why would an optimizing agent—God—not have made men such that they always freely choose the good?"[5] And then there are the calls for acknowledging that of course there could be such a world—one devoid of imperfect creatures like you and me. (It is surely not all that pleasant to think that the world would be a better place without us!) However, the Leibnizian answer does good service here in its observation that while God could indeed have created such a world, the result would not have been as good overall, everything considered— that, thanks to the intricate interconnection of things in a systemic world-reality, the comparative price to be paid by replacing imperfect humanity with angels would be unacceptable because erasing one sort of imperfection from the world-picture nevertheless engenders a more than compensating imperfection elsewhere (say by eliminating from the scheme of things any prospect of moral growth, repentance, and atonement).[6]

Such lines of reasoning can, in principle, account for the *existence* of moral and physical evil even in a world that is favorable to the welfare of intelligent beings. However, a further and more difficult problem looms, namely the question not just of why there is *some* evil in the world but rather why there is *so much* of it.

The sensible response to theorists of the "I could design it better than this" school is to process the question: how do you propose to effect these improvements? Basically there are two options:

1. by *replacement* of (some part of) what is there

2. by *emendation* of (some part of) what is there

Now at this point it is well to heed the teachings of Leibniz, who insists that it is the entire history of a thing in this world that defines and individuates it as what it indeed is, so that (2) is in effect tantamount to (1).[7]

Accordingly, to improve the world requires repopulating it with different agents whose choices are indeed appropriate. In the end, it would mean repopulating reality with angels so as to engender a world without morally imperfect agents. Such a world would doubtless be a better world. But would it be *for the better* that such a world still exists instead of ours?

Here, we arrive at a subtle but important point, namely that it is emphatically not the same thing to say:

- World *A* is better than world *B*

- It is for the better that world *A* should exist rather than world *B*

This raises delicate issues that require a closer look.

The most promising line of thought that is available here was pioneered in Leibniz's own theodicidic reflections:

- That a world should exist—that some world or other should actually be there—is rationally desirable in view of the consideration that there are some possible worlds whose overall positive/negative balance is favorable in that their positivities outweigh their negativities.

- If there is to be a world, then it is rationally desirable that this should be the best of realizable positivities—that is, it should be such that no other possibility outranks it in point of an overall positive/negative balance.

On this basis, the world as it is—multitudinous evils included—is not outranked by any other competitor among the realizable possibilities.

Accordingly, even the very best of possible world arrangements need not and will not call for being *perfect*. What matters here is, thanks to the inherent and unavoidable interconnection of things in a complex world, it may transpire that the only possible way to achieve a diminution of negativity at one point demands a more than compensatory argumentation of negativity at another. Even the best of possible worlds can admit all manner of imperfections: it is just a matter of there being fewer of them, on balance, than is the case with any of the other alternatives.

Dr. Pangloss' anxious pupil pressed him with the question, "If this is the best of all possible worlds, what are the others like?"[8] And here, a perfectly good answer was available to the good doctor, which despite its cogency he was reluctant to give, namely the reply: "Even worse!" The facile optimism of Dr. Pangloss, the butt of Voltaire's *Candide*, misses the mark if Leibniz (and not some naive and simple-minded Leibnizian) is intended as its target. Optimalism, to reemphasize, is not really a matter of unqualified optimism.

15

Why Philosophy?

It is one of the ironies of twentieth-century philosophy that self-distrust pervades the entire enterprise. The era's schools of thought, otherwise the most varied and reciprocally discordant views, seem to agree on one—and perhaps only one—significant point: that the discipline as traditionally understood and historically cultivated is misguided, profoundly wrong, and in crying need of abandonment. With remarkable unanimity, the philosophers of the twentieth century have wanted to replace philosophy as traditionally practiced by something else. Science, logic, linguistics of some sort, history of ideas, sociology, and cultural studies have all figured among one theorist or another's favored successors. Virtually no one has been content to have philosophy continue doing business as usual.

In the century's course, this sort of anti-philosophical view has become pervasive. Martin Heidegger spoke disdainfully of traditional metaphysics as "a mere vestige of Christian theology." And we find comparably dismissive postures in logical positivism, in Wittgenstein, in various versions of pragmatism, in analytic philosophy, especially in ordinary language philosophy, and in Karl Marx's insistence that while philosophy's historic mission has been to understand the world, the real task is to change it. And then too there is the so-called quietism of such contemporary Wittgenstein-inspired philosophers as Cora Diamond and John McDowell.[1]

As an incidental aside, it deserves remark that the term *quietism* is a singularly unfortunate choice for the sceptical position at issue, given the established usage of that expression. Here is what the recent *Dictionary of Philosophy and Religion* has to say about what quietism involves:

> [A] 17th-century devotional and mystical movement within the Catholic Church . . . The movement held that the path to the discovery of the Divine Will required one to "sell or kill" one's self-conscious will. One's whole soul may thus be directed to the love of God. "Waiting on God" through meditation became central. A Quietist maxim held that one moment's contemplation is worth a thousand years' good works.[2]

Now, whatever the antiphilosophical position of those latter-day, so-called quietists may have in mind, it is surely not a matter of prioritizing contemplative meditation over good works.

But issues of terminology aside, the problem with the dismissive treatment of philosophy is that it fails to do justice to the consideration that philosophizing is effectively indispensable within the broader context of rational inquiry. And the point is perhaps most persuasively made obliquely—through concrete examples rather than directly through the general principles they instantiate.

So let us begin with an example from epistemology. Consider the following three contentions:

1. Claims to factual knowledge are sometimes rationally appropriate.

2. For rational appropriateness, the specifics of factual knowledge must always be certain. (It makes no sense to say, "I know that *p* is the case, but there is some shadow of doubt about it [or: it may fail to be so].")

3. Claims to absolute, indubitable certainty are never rationally warranted and appropriate.

The trouble with this trio is that its contentions are logically inconsistent. Mere rationality accordingly demands that least one or the other of its contentions must be rejected. And no matter which way we turn, we will become enmeshed in a venture of substantive philosophizing. For in rejecting such a thesis as unacceptable, we effectively ally ourselves to its negation. And so consider:

1–*rejection*	Claims to factual knowledge are never rationally appropriate. (Scepticism)
2–*rejection*	Factual knowledge need not be certain. (Cognitive Fallibilism)
3–*rejection*	Claims to absolute and indubitable certainty are sometimes appropriate. (Cataleptic Evidentism)

We come up against a fixed choice. And in every case, we are in effect caught up in the grasp of one or another tried-and-true philosophical position.

And this sort of thing is quite general. Thus, consider the following group of contentions:

1. All occurrences in nature, human acts included, are causally determined.

2. Humans can and do act freely on occasion.

3. A genuinely free act cannot be causally determined—for if it were so determined, then the act would not be free by virtue of this very circumstance.

What we have here is another inconsistent group whose resolution is open to various alternatives:

1–*rejection*	A "voluntaristic" exemption of free acts from the web of causal determination. (Descartes)
2–*rejection*	A "deterministic" subjection of the human will to causal constraints. (Spinoza)
3–*rejection*	A "compatibilism" of free action and causal determination—for example, via a theory that distinguishes between inner and outer causal

determination, and sees the former as compatible with freedom. (Leibniz)

Of course, while one or the other of those rejections is mandatory, there remains a wide latitude of options with respect to the rationale through which this step is going to be accounted for. (Those philosopher-indicated, philosophical positions are mere examples of the sort of story that could be told here.) But the key fact remains that no matter what sort of account one is prepared to give, the story being told will be told in the way of philosophy. Whatever sort of rationale we offer for that rejection is going to be philosophical in its nature and bearing.

Or again, consider yet another example:

1. Acting unjustly is always impermissible.

2. In some—inherently dilemmatic—circumstances an unjust action is unavoidable.

3. An act that is unavoidable (in the circumstances) cannot be impermissible (in those circumstances).

Here too, we have an inconsistent triad. A rational person cannot but abandon one or the other of them. But in view of their supposed rationality, our rejector will be committed to acting for a reason. Their very rationality binds them to having some sort of rationale for their proceeding. And once the rejector offers an explanatory rationale for this rejection, he or she is doing philosophy.

Thus, for example, we might have the following situation:

1–*rejection*	Acting unjustly is sometimes permissible. The least of evils is always permissible, and in suitably unfortunate circumstances, this least of evils can involve some element of injustice.
2–*rejection*	The realizability of just action is never unavailable. The best available alternative for acting can never count as unjust.
3–*rejection*	An act that is unavoidable can indeed be impermissible. There can be moral dilemmas that force a choice between impermissible acts.

And in each case, the rationale at issue provides for an enmeshment in what cannot but count as a philosophical position.

So here is the situation. For starters, we are confronted with a group of collectively incompatible propositions. And these propositions can be devoid of any transparent philosophical involvement. But given their collective inconsistency, one or the other of them has to go. And providing a plausible rationale for the specific rejection of any particular one of them is inevitably going to involve deliberations of the sort that are quintessentially philosophical.

To be sure, faced with the imperative of rejection in such cases, a theorist may go all-out and take the following line:

> I shall never accept anything because no contention is ever acceptable. (Scepticism)

Or perhaps somewhat more restrictedly:

> I shall never accept anything that has any bearing on philosophical matters. (Since virtually every fact has some degree of philosophical relevancy, this sort of scepticism has a tendency to transmute into the preceding, seemingly more radical sort.)

Now, when any position along such lines is rendered rational by being fitted out with a plausible rationale of some sort, then we at once find ourselves back at philosophizing—deeply engaged in the epistemology of rational acceptance. And we then face the problem that the sort of broadcast approach represented by that envisioned reaction is not really appropriate because the rejection of *specific* contentions of the sort at issue in our apories calls for the deployment of case-specific consideration. In matters of specific rejection, a wholesale approach through guilt by association will hardly be justifiable. Those sceptical antiphilosophers effectively say:

> A plague in all your houses. The very philosophical bearing (oblique or otherwise) that those inconsistent clusters involve brings all of these conflicting theses within the scope of my antiphilosophical proscription. I thus reject the whole lot of them without further ado or scrutiny. I see no reason to confront them individually in their idiosyncratic detail.

However, this seemingly plausible stance fails to meet the needs of the situation. For the very dialectic of rational controversy precludes this tactic. Consider an illustration. You say: "All Cretans are liars." I present you with a particular Cretan and say: "This man is no liar." There is now no longer any option but to look into the mouth of this particular gift horse. It will no longer do to remain at the level of wholesale generality and say: "But he is a Cretan and all Cretans are liars." It is exactly this sort of generalization that is in question.

The fact of it is that the dialectic of rational controversy prioritizes specifics over generalities.[3] In this sort of situation, presumption stands on the side of the particular and the burden of proof rests on the side of generality. So the antiphilosopher has no viable excuse for refusing to engage the details of particular cases.

The overall lesson is as follows: If you are going to be rational, then you are bound to confront some contentions that you cannot but reject, and these contentions are such that the moment you try to provide *grounds* for rejection and set out some sort of *rationale* for it, then—like it or not—you are going to be involved in philosophizing. Philosophy, that is to say, is effectively unavoidable in the rational scheme of things as long as we engage in the quest for cogent answers to large questions.

There is, of course, the theoretical possibility of taking the stance that was indeed advocated by some of the leading sceptics of classical antiquity: namely, that of living *adoxustos* (without doctrine), going along in life doing all sorts of things without worrying about the rhyme or reason of it, following the drift of inclination, habit, or custom. Effectively, one says: "I have better things to do than to concern myself about the reasons for what I do or think." This is, no doubt, a stance one can possibly take, and there are doubtless many people who take it. But it is clear that such an abandonment of reason is not a stance that is *rationally* defensible. It is not that people cannot refrain from philosophizing, but rather that rational people really have no cogent grounds for urging such abandonment.

NOTES

1. The Task of Philosophy

1. Aristotle, *Metaphysics*, 928b10.

2. There are, of course, very different ways of *doing* philosophy even as there are different ways of cooking food. But the enterprise itself is characterized by its defining objective: if one isn't doing that sort of thing, then one isn't pursuing it. (Sewing is not cooking food, nor is journalism philosophy.)

3. William James, "The Sentiment of Rationality," in *The Will to Believe and other Essays in Popular Philosophy* (New York: Longmans Green, 1897), 63–110, see esp. 78–79.

4. Quoted in *Aristotelis Fragmenta Selecta*, ed. W. D. Ross (Oxford: Clarendon Press, 1955), vii; for the text see page 28. But see also Anton-Hermann Chroust, *Aristotle, Protrepicus: A Reconstruction* (Notre Dame: University of Notre Dame Press, 1969), 48–50.

5. F. H. Bradley, *Appearance and Reality*, 2nd ed. (Oxford: Clarendon Press, 1897), 1.

6. Paul K. Feyerabend embraces the concurrent use of mutually inconsistent scientific theories within a "theoretical pluralism." See his essay, "Problems of Empiricism" in *Beyond the Edge of Certainty*, ed. R. G. Colodny (Englewood Cliffs, NJ: Prentice-Hall, 1965), 145–260, see esp. 164–68.

7. John Kekes, *The Nature of Philosophy* (Totowa, NJ: Rowman & Littlefield, 1980), 196.

2. Knowledge and Scepticism

1. His clear awareness of this made it possible for the Platonic Academy to endorse scepticism throughout the middle phase of its development in classical antiquity.

2. Thus one acute thinker has written:

> [W]hat are my grounds for thinking that I, in my own particular case, shall die. I am as certain of it in my innermost mind, as I am that I now live; but what is the distinct evidence on which I allow myself to be certain? How would I tell it in a court of justice? How should I fare under a cross-examination upon the grounds of my certitude?·Demonstration of course I cannot have of a future event. (J. H. Newman, *A Grammar of Assent*, [London and New York: Longmans, Green, 1913], chap. 8, pt. 2, sect. I.)

3. Bertrand Russell, *Problems of Philosophy* (Oxford: Oxford University Press, 1912), 35.

4. It must be realized that the "certainty" at issue in these discussions is not the subjective psychological stare of a *feeling* of certainly at issue in locutions like "I *feel* certain that *p*." Rather it is a matter of the objective epistemic circumstances, and the relevant locutions are of the impersonal character of "I is certain that *p*." This is crucial to the sceptic's case, "And once we have noticed this distinction, we are forced to allow what we are certain of is very much less than we should have said otherwise." (H. A. Pritchard, *Knowledge and Perception* [Oxford: Oxford University Press, 1930], 97.)

5. As Keith Lehrer has put it:

> [I]t should also be clear why it is that ordinary men commonly, though incorrectly, believe that they know for certain that some contingent statements are true. They believe that there is no chance whatever that they are wrong in thinking some contingent statements are true and thus feel sure they know for certain that those statements are true. One reason they feel sure is that they have not reflected upon the ubiquity of . . . change in all human thought. Once these matters are brought into focus, we may reasonably conclude that no man knows for certain that any contingent statement is true. ("Scepticism and Conceptual Change" in *Empirical Knowledge*, eds. R. M. Chisholm and R. J. Swartz, (Englewood Cliffs, NJ: Prentice Hall, 1973), 47–58, see esp. 53.)

In a similar vein, L. S. Carrier has recently argued, in effect, that since belief concerning material objects can in theory turn out to be mistaken, no one ever knows that he knows such a belief to be true. See his "Scepticism Made Certain," *Journal of Philosophy* 71 (1974): 140–50.

6. For scepticism and its critique, see Robert Audi, *Belief, Justification, and Knowledge* (Belmont, CA: Wadsworth, 1988); A. I. Goldman, *Epistemology and Cognition* (Cambridge: Harvard University Press, 1986); Peter Klein, *Certainty:*

A Refutation of Scepticism (Minneapolis: University of Minnesota Press, 1981); Keith Lehrer, *Knowledge* (Oxford: Oxford University Press, 1974); Robert Nozick, *Philosophical Explanations* (Cambridge: Harvard University Press, 1981); and Peter Unger, *Ignorance: A Case for Scepticism* (Oxford: Clarendon Press, 1975); as well as the author's *Scepticism: A Critical Reappraisal* (Oxford: Basil Blackwell, 1980), which gives extensive references to the literature.

7. The "problem of knowledge" that figures in much of the epistemological literature is thus a creation of those philosophers who endow our knowledge claims with a hyperbolic absoluteness never envisaged in or countenanced by our ordinary usage of knowledge-terminology. Having initially created difficulties by distorting our usage, philosophers are then at great pains to try to revalidate it. This whole project gives an aura of unrealism to much of epistemological discussion. For an interesting discussion of relevant issues, see Oliver A. Johnson, *The Problem of Knowledge* (The Hague: Martinus Nijhoff, 1974).

8. On this issue, see J. L. Austin in "Other Minds" (1946), reprinted in his *Philosophical Papers* (Oxford: Clarendon Press, 1961), 44–84. To be sure, the operation of the distinction between realistic and hyperbolic possibilities of error will to some extent depend upon "the state of 'knowledge' of the day." But this simply carries us back to the truism that what people reasonably accept as known is state-of-knowledge dependent, and the plausibly purported knowledge of one era may turn out to be the error of another.

9. Compare to Harry G. Frankfurt, "Philosophical Certainly," *Philosophical Review* 71 (1962): 303–27. However, the philosopher (unlike the natural scientist) is simply not free to switch over to "technical terms." His task is to elucidate the concepts we actually work with, and in replacing them by technical reconstructions, he merely changes the subject.

10. As William James said:

[Someone] who says "Better to go without belief forever than believe a lie!" merely shows his own preponderant private horror of becoming a dupe. . . . But I can believe that worse things than being duped may happen to a man in this world. (*The Will to Believe*, [New York: Longmans, Green, and Co., 1897], 18–19)

11. C. S. Peirce, *Collected Papers*, Vol. II (Cambridge: Harvard University Press, 1931), sect. 2.112.

12. Further issues relevant to some of this chapter's themes are discussed in the author's *Scepticism: A Critical Reappraisal* (Oxford: Basil Blackwell, 1980).

3. Limits of Science

1. The author's *Cognitive Systematization: A Systems-Theoretic Approach to a Coherentist Theory of Knowledge* (Oxford: Blackwell, 1979) deals with these matters, as does *The Limits of Science* (Pittsburgh: University of Pittsburgh Press, 1999).

2. Note that this is independent of the question, "Would we ever want to do so?" Do we ever want to answer all those predictive questions about ourselves and our environment, or are we more comfortable in the condition in which "ignorance is bliss"?

3. S. W. Hawking, "Is the End in Sight for Theoretical Physics?" *Physics Bulletin* 32 (1981): 15–17.

4. This sentiment was abroad among physicists of the *fin de siècle* era of 1890–1900, see Lawrence Badash, "The Completeness of Nineteenth-Century Science," *Isis* 63 (1972): 48–58. And such sentiments are coming back into fashion today, see Richard Feynmann, *The Character of Physical Law* (Cambridge: MIT Press, 1965), 172. See also Gunther Stent, *The Coming of the Golden Age* (Garden City, N.Y.: Natural History Press, 1969); and S. W. Hawking, "Is the End in Sight for Theoretical Physics?" *Physics Bulletin* 32 (1981): 15–17.

5. See Eber Jeffrey, "Nothing Left to Invent," *Journal of the Patent Office Society* 22 (July 1940): 479–81.

6. For this inference could only be made if we could move from a thesis of the format $\sim(\exists r)(r \, \varepsilon S \, \& \, r \oslash p)$ to one of the format $(\exists r)(r \, \varepsilon S \, \& \, r \oslash \sim p)$, where "$\oslash$" represents a grounding relationship of "furnishing a good reason" and p is, in this case, the particular thesis, "S will at some point require drastic revision." That is, the inference would go through only if the lack (in S) of a good reason for p were itself to assure the existence (in S) of a good reason for $\sim p$. But the transition to this conclusion from the given premise would go through only if the former antecedent fact itself constituted such a good reason, that is, only if we have $\sim(\exists r)(r \, \varepsilon S \, \& \, r \oslash p)\oslash \sim p$. Thus, the inference would go through only if, by the contraposition, $p \oslash(\exists r)(r \, \varepsilon S \, \& \, r \oslash p)$. This thesis claims that the vary truth of p will itself be a good reason to hold that S affords a good reason for p—in sum, that S is complete.

7. Some of the issues of this discussion are developed at greater length in the author's *Methodological Pragmatism: Systems-Theoretic Approach to the Theory of Knowledge* (Oxford: Blackwell, 1977), *Scientific Progress: A Philosophical Essay on the Economics of Research in Natural Science* (Oxford: Blackwell, 1979), and *Cognitive Systematization* (Oxford: Blackwell, 1979).

8. On the theme of this chapter see also the author's *Ethical Idealism: An Inquiry into the Nature and Function of Ideals* (Berkeley and Los Angeles: University of California Press, 1987), esp. chap. 6, "The Power of Ideals."

4. Realism/Idealism

1. Bertrand Russell, *The Problems of Philosophy* (Oxford: Clarendon Press, 1912), 58.

2. The author's involvement with the defense of this version of idealism goes back to his *Conceptual Idealism* (Oxford: Basil Blackwell, 1973).

5. Intelligent Design

1. The neo-Platonists Plotinus and Proclus differentiated natural *phusikôs* love (*amor naturalis*), and psychic (*psychikôs*) love (*amor sensitivus*) from intellectual love: *erôs noerôs* (*amor intellectualis* or *rationalis*). In the end, their rendition of the Aristotelian idea that "love makes the world go round" comes down to having a world developed conformably and sympathetically to the demands of the intellect in relation to intelligibility.

2. The most eloquent exponent of nootropism is Teilhard de Chardin. Whether the evolutionary emergence of what he calls the noosphere will go as far as to reach the ultimate "omega state" that he envisions could be seen as speculative and eschatological. Yet the fundamental process of ratiotropic evolution that he envisions is there for all to see presently, irrespective of how far they may be prepared to venture into its speculative projection into a yet uncertain future. While in their detail the present deliberations differ substantially from those of Teilhard, nevertheless their tendency and motivating spirit is unquestionably akin to his.

3. See William S. Dembski, *The Design Inference: Eliminating Chance Through Small Probabilities* (Cambridge: Cambridge University Press, 1998). The quarrel between orthodox Darwinians and Intelligent Design Theorists of the more conservative stamp is not over the question of evolution by chance selection but simply over the question of whether such selection is strictly random or bias-manifestly skewed. What is at issue here is not a choice between science versus religion but choice between two rival scientific theories.

4. As regards the Catholic ramifications of the issue, it is certainly true that the Church emphasizes the distinction between body and soul, and it views the former, soul, not as a product of the physical causality of nature but of a special act of creation on the part of God. But this of course need not (and indeed should not) be construed as creating an unmendable breach between doctrine and evolution, since there simply is no need to claim that evolution creates souls rather than saying that it affords fitting occasions for the creation of souls.

6. Fallacies Regarding Free Will

1. Daniel Dennett, "I Could not Have Done Otherwise—So What," *Journal of Philosophy* 81 (1984): 553–65 (my italics). Compare to Dennett, *Elbow Room: The Varieties of Free Will Worth Wanting* (Cambridge: MIT Press, 1984), 16.

2. Note that while predetermination entails precedence determination, the converse is not the case: precedence determination does not entail predetermination.

3. "Das wahre Causalprincip steht . . . der Freiheit nicht im Wege," in Lotze, *Microcosmus: An Essay Concerning Man and His Relation to the World*, vol. I (New York: Scribner & Welford, 1890), 16.

4. Daniel Dennett, *Freedom Evolves* (New York: Viking, 2003), 120.

5. Ibid.

6. Spinoza, *Ethics*, Book I, Appendix.

7. Lotze, *Microcosmus: An Essay Concerning Man and His Relation to the World*, vol. I (New York: Scribner & Welford, 1890), 287.

7. Mind and Matter

1. Theodore Honderich, ed., *Essays on Freedom of Action* (London: Routledge, 1973), 189. However the author emphatically declines to take a position on the issue of whether brain state causes the mind state (190), and also passes the reverse idea over in discrete silence. But it is just this prospect—not so much of *causation* as of state-change *initiation*—that lies at the heart of the present deliberations.

2. Moritz Schlick, *Problems of Ethics* (New York: Dover Publications, 1962), chap. 8.

3. On mind-brain interaction, see Jürgen Boeck's "Bietet die Gehirnforschung Einblick in Freiräume menschlichen und tierischen Verhaltens," in *Aspekte der Freiheit*, ed. Dieter Henrich, 9–22 (Regensburg: Mittelbayerische Druckerei- u. Verlagsgesellschaft, 1982).

4. There are a vast number of fine books on the subject. A random sampling includes, John C. Eccles, *How the Self Controls its Brain* (Berlin: Springer, 1994); Theodore Honderich, *A Theory of Determinism*, 2 vols. (Oxford: Clarendon, 1990); Gary Watson, ed., *Free Will* (Oxford: Oxford University Press, 1982).

5. R. H. Lotze, "Das Verhältnis der Seele zum Leib ist stets das einer Herrschaft," in *Medizinische Psychologie oder Physiologie der Seele* (Leipzig, 1852), 289.

6. See Immanuel Kant, *Critique of Pure Reason*, A803 = B831.

7. The reverse will not of course be the case.

8. Dickinson Miller writing as R. E. Hobart, "Free Will as Involving Determination and Inconceivable Without it," *Mind* 43, no. 169 (1934): 1–27.

9. John Stuart Mill's *A System of Logic* (London: John W. Parker, West Strand, 1843) is one of the earliest works that is altogether sound on the issues of this paragraph.

8. Pragmatism and Practical Rationality

1. And what other view point would it possibly make sense for us to adopt here?

2. Other aspects of the presently deliberated issues are treated in the author's *Rationality* (Oxford: Oxford University Press, 1986).

3. The issue goes back to the specification of the "basics" (*principiae*) of the human good in the Middle Academy (Carneades)—things like the soundness and maintenance of the members of the body, health, sound senses, freedom from pain, physical vigor, and physical attractiveness. Compare with Cicero, *De finibus*, V. vii. 19.

4. For strict consistency, a rigorous Humean should, by analogy, hold that cognitive reason too is only hypothetical—that it only tells us that certain beliefs must be abandoned *if* we hold certain others, and that no beliefs are contrary to reason as such, so that "it is not contrary to reason to think one's finger larger than the entire earth."

5. Further issues relevant to this chapter's deliberations are discussed in the author's *The Validity of Values: Human Values in Pragmatic Perspective* (Princeton: Princeton University Press, 1993).

9. The Demands of Morality

1. It is to the credit of the utilitarian tradition that it has stressed this gearing of morality to the benefit of people, for it clearly establishes the issues as subject to rational deliberation. But it is to its discredit that it has seen these benefits in terms of pleasure and mere personal preference alone, so that the veneer of rationality is very thin indeed.

2. Compare to J. N. Findlay, *Language, Mind and Value* (London: Allen & Unwyn, 1963), chaps. 5 and 6.

3. Though their choices do affect how these interests operate. Once you have chosen Helen to be your future wife, her attitude towards you becomes a matter of substantial interest for you.

4. Does this way of viewing the matter put subrational, salient actions outside the pale of moral concern? By no means. For it matters deeply to rational agents how other rational agents treat animals—or for that matter any other sorts of beings that have interests capable of being injured. We have a substantial interest in how others comport themselves who also belong to the type that we see ourselves as belonging to.

5. But just who are the "we" at issue. Clearly, those who are members of our linguistic community—those who realize that when we speak of "morality" we mean *morality* (with the various things involved therein), and not, say, basket weaving.

6. The analogy of natural law is helpful: "Theft, murder, adultery and all injuries are forbidden by the laws of nature; but which is to be called theft, what murder, what adultery, what injury in a citizen, this is not to be determined by the natural but by the civil law." (Thomas Hobbes, *De Cive*, chap. IV, sect. 16). St. Thomas holds that appropriate human law must be subordinate to the natural law by way of "particular determination," with different human laws, varying from place to place, nevertheless representing appropriate concretizations of the same underlying principle of natural law (See *Summa Theologica*, IaIIae, questions 95–96).

7. Aspects of these issues are helpfully discussed in Susan Wolf, "Two Levels of Pluralism," *Ethics* 102 (1992): 785–98.

8. After all, "the actual variations in the moral code (of different groups) are more readily explained by the hypothesis that they reflect different ways of life

than by the hypothesis that they express perceptions, most of them seriously inadequate and badly distorted, of objective values" (J. L. Mackie, *Ethics: Inventing Right and Wrong* [Hammondsworth: Penguin Books, 1977], 37).

9. Stephen L. Darwall, *Impartial Reason* (Ithaca, NY: Cornell University Press, 1983), 105.

10. Further issues relevant to some of this chapter's themes are discussed in the author's *Moral Absolutes: An Essay on the Nature and Rationale of Morality* (New York: Peter Lang, 1989).

11. To be sure, someone may ask: "Why think of ourselves in this way—why see ourselves as free rational agents?" But of course to ask this is to ask for a good rational reason and is thus already to take a stance within the framework of rationality. In theory, one can of course "resign" from the community of rational beings, abandoning all claims to being more than "mere animals." But this is a step one cannot *justify*—there are no satisfactory rational grounds for taking it. And this is something most of us realize instinctively. The appropriateness of acknowledging others as responsible agents whenever possible holds in our own case as well.

12. Immanuel Kant portrayed the obligation at issue in the following terms:

First, it is one's duty to raise himself out of the crudity of his nature—out of his animality (*quoad actum*) more and more to humanity, by which alone he is capable of setting himself ends. It is man's [paramount] duty to . . . supply by instruction what is lacking in his knowledge, and to correct his mistakes. . . .[T]his end [is] his duty in order that he may . . . be worthy of the humanity dwelling within him. (*Metaphysics of Morals*, 387, Akad.)

10. By Whose Standards?

1. See Immanuel Kant, *Foundations in the Metaphysics of Minds*, trans. Lewis White Beck (Indianapolis and New York: Bobbs Merril, 1959).

2. William James was surely right to insist that, "There is no point of view absolutely public and universal" (*Talks to Teachers on Psychology* [New York: Henry Regnery, 1899], 4).

11. Pluralism and Concretization Quandaries

1. The author's *Pluralism: Against the Demand for Consensus* (Oxford: Clarendon Press, 1993), offers further perspectives on some of the themes of this chapter.

12. The Power of Ideals

1. J. O. Urmson, "Saints and Heroes," in *Essays in Moral Philosophy*, ed. A. I. Melden (Seattle: University of Washington Press, 1958). On this theme, see also David Heyd, *Supererogation: Its Status in Ethical Theory* (Cambridge: Cambridge University Press, 1984).

2. "Nicht minder richtig aber ist, dass das Mögliche sehr oft nur dadurch erreicht wurde, dass man nach dem jenseits seiner Kraft liegenden Unmöglichen griff." Max Weber, "Der Sinn der 'Wertfreiheit' in den soziologischen und ökonomischen Wissenschaften," *Logos* 7 (1917–18): 63; reprinted in *Gesammelte Aufsätze zur Wissenschaftslehre* (Tübingen: J. C. B. Mohr, 1922), 476.

3. Aldous Huxley, "Inquiry into the Nature of Ideals and the Methods Employed for Their Realization," in *Ends and Means* (London: Chatto & Windus, 1937), 1.

4. L. Susan Stebbing, *Ideals and Illusions* (London: Watts & Co., 1948), 132–33.

5. Further issues relevant to some of this chapter's themes are discussed in the author's *Ethical Idealism: A Study of the Import of Ideals* (Berkeley, Los Angeles, London: University of California Press, 1987).

13. Science and Religion

This chapter is dedicated to my daughter Catherine, who encouraged me to discuss the question that it addresses. I am grateful to Robert Kaita, James V. Maher, and Aug Tong for constructive suggestions.

1. William James, *The Varieties of Religious Experience* (New York & London: Longmans Green, 1902), 487.

2. Reading Blaise Pascal's *Thoughts* (*Pensées*) may give you good guidance here! And a vast body of excellent material is available on the topic of this chapter. Michael Ruse's *Can a Darwinian be a Christian* (Cambridge: Cambridge University Press, 2001) is a good example. A fine contemporary anthology is A. R. Peacock's *The Sciences and Theology in the Twentieth Century* (Notre Dame: Notre Dame University Press, 1985). The Web site of the American Scientific Affiliation (ASA): A Fellowship of Christians in Science (http://www.asa3. org/asa/topics/empty/WebList/List1WebBooks.html) points to many excellent discussions of these topics. Some stimulating deliberations are offered in the personal statements of Francis S. Collins's *The Language of God: A Scientist Presents Evidence for Belief* (New York: Free Press, 2006) and Owen Gingerich's *God's Universe* (Cambridge: Harvard University Press, 2006). An interesting collection of interviews with twelve leading scientists is presented in P. Clayton and J. Schaal's *Practicing Science, Living Faith* (New York: Columbia University Press, 2007). Two scholarly journals of excellent quality are devoted to cognate issues: *Faith and Philosophy* and *Zygon: Journal of Religion and Science*. The Templeton Foundation has sponsored numberless conferences and workshops for constructive interchange between scientists and theologians. Many scientific investigators are nowadays pursuing lines of research that have religious ramifications. An example of a scientifically sophisticated paper of theological bearing, whose general drift, at least, may be accessible to a scientifically untutored reader, is Euan J. Squires, "Do We Live in the Simplest Possible Interesting World?" *The European Journal of Physics* 2 (1981): 55–57.

14. On the Improvability of the World

1. See, for example, R. K. Perkins, Jr., "An Atheistic Argument from the Improvability of the Universe," *Nous* 17 (1983): 239–50.

2. *Timaeus*, 29E–30B (emphasis added).

3. Dr. Seuss, *Happy Birthday to You* (New York: Random House Children's Books, 1959), 10.

4. Edward Norton Lorenz, "Deterministic Nonperiodic Flow," *Journal of Atmospheric Sciences* 20 (1963): 130–41.

5. See J. L. Mackie, "Freedom and Omnipotence," *Mind* 64 (1955): 200–12.

6. Mackie's preference for a totally sinless world overlooks the fact that the Catholic theology has long characterized the sin of Adam as a *felix culpa*—a fortunate sin—because it paved the way to the entire arena of atonement and salvation.

7. Leibniz holds that it is erroneous to think "I could have chosen otherwise." Had that choice come out differently, it would not have been *you* who did so but yet another closely similar individual: the choice difference would ipso facto engender a difference in the chooser.

8. Voltaire, *Candide*, chap. iv. For a better understanding of Leibniz's stance, see his *Discourse on Metaphysics*, sec. 6; *Principle of Nature and of Grace*, sec. 10; and *Theodicée*, sec. 208.

15. Why Philosophy?

1. The use of the term quietism to characterize Wittgenstein's antiphilosophical position apparently became current in Oxford during the 1970s with such philosophers as Crispin Wright, Simon Blackburn, and Nick Zangwill. It has been enroute to transmutation from Wittgensteinian exegesis to outright advocacy in such neo-Wittgensteinian philosophers as Cora Diamond and John McDowell. See David G. Stern, *Wittgenstein's Philosophical Investigations* (Cambridge: Cambridge University Press, 2004), 168–70.

2. W. L. Reese, ed., *Dictionary of Philosophy and Religion* (Atlantic Highlands, NJ: Humanities Press, 1980), 628.

3. Further issues relevant to some of this chapter's themes are discussed in the author's *Conditionals* (Cambridge: MIT Press, 2007).

INDEX OF NAMES

Aristotle, 8, 10, 33, 34, 63, 108, 207n1
Audi, Robert, 208n6
Austin, J. L., 209n8
Ayer, A. J., ix

Badash, Lawrence, 210n4
Bartolomeo de las Casas, 149
Berkeley, George, 94
Blackburn, Simon, 216n1 (chap. 15)
Boeck, Jürgen, 212n3 (chap. 7)
Bradley, F. H., 8, 207n5

Carneades, 212n3 (chap. 8)
Carrier, L. S., 208n5
Chardin, Teilhard de, 211n2 (chap. 5)
Chroust, Anton-Hermann, 207n4
Cicero, 212n3 (chap. 8)
Clayton, Philip, 215n2 (chap. 13)
Collins, Francis S., 215n2 (chap. 13)

Darwall, Stephen, 214n9
Darwin, Charles, 180
Dembski, William S., 211n3 (chap. 5)
Dennett, Daniel, 74, 211n1 (chap. 6), 211n4 (chap. 6)
Descartes, René, 20, 96, 203
Diamond, Cora, 202, 216n1 (chap. 15)
Dr. Seuss, 71, 190, 216n3 (chap. 14)

Eccles, John C., 212n4
Einstein, Albert, 160, 179
Emerson, R. W., 183

Feyerabend, Paul K., 207n6
Feynmann, Richard, 210n4 (chap. 3)
Findlay, J. N., 213n2
Frankfurt, Harry G., 209n9

Galileo, Galilei, 160, 179
Gasset, Ortega y, 52

Gingerich, Owen, 215n2 (chap. 13)
Goldman, A. I., 208n6

Hawking, S. W., 210n3, 210n4
Hegel, G. W. F., 40, 147
Heidegger, Martin, 201
Heyd, David, 214n1 (chap. 12)
Hitler, Adolf, 140, 191
Hobbes, Thomas, 94, 213n6
Homer, 182
Honderich, Theodore, 212n4
Hume, David, 96
Huxley, Aldous, 163–64, 215n3
    (chap. 12)

Jacobs, W. W., 194
James, William, 4, 14, 183, 207n3,
    209n10, 214n2 (chap. 10), 215n1
Jeffrey, Eber, 210n5
Johnson, Oliver A., 209n7

Kaita, Robert, 215n (chap. 13)
Kant, Immanuel, 39, 95, 137, 187, 197,
    212n6 (chap. 7), 214n12 (chap. 9),
    214n1 (chap. 10)
Kekes, John, 207n7
Khrushchev, Nikita, 177
Klein, Peter, 208n6

La Mettrie, J. O. de, 94
Laplace, Pierre-Simon marquis de,
    94, 173, 176, 189
Lehrer, Keith, 208n5, 208–9n6
Leibniz, G. W., 190, 194, 196, 199–200,
    204, 216n8, 216n9
Lincoln, Abraham, 185
Lorenz, Edward Norton, 192, 216n4
Lotze, R. H., 94, 211n3 (chap. 6),
    212n7 (chap. 6), 212n5 (chap. 7)

Mackie, J. L., 213–14n8, 216n5, 216n6
Maher, James V., 215n (chap. 13)
Marx, Karl, 147, 163, 202
Maxwell, James Clark, 33, 179
McDowell, John, 202, 216n1 (chap.
    15)
Mill, John Stuart, 150, 212n9
Miller, Dickinson, (R. E. Hobert), 95,
    212n8

Newman, J. H., 183, 208n2
Newton, Isaac, 33, 179
Nicholas of Cusa, 11
Nozick, Robert, 208–9n6

Pascal, Blaise, 215n2 (chap. 13)
Peirce, Charles Sanders, 33, 45,
    209n11
Perkins, R. K., 216n1 (chap. 14)
Plato, 20, 63, 189–90
Plotinus, 63, 211n1 (chap. 5)
Prichard, H. A., 208n4
Proclus, 63, 211n1 (chap. 5)
Ptolemy, 33
Pusey, 183

Rescher, Catherine, 215n (chap. 13)
Ruse, Michael, 215n2 (chap. 13)
Russell, Bertrand, ix, 52, 208n3,
    210n1

Santayana, 57
Schaal, J., 215n2 (chap. 13)
Schlick, Mortiz, 92, 212n2 (chap. 7)
Schopenhauer, 57
Socrates, 3, 94
Spinoza, 85, 203, 212n6 (chap. 6)
Squires, Euan J., 215n2 (chap. 15)
Stalin, 140, 160, 191
Stebbing, Susan, 163–64, 215n4

Stent, Gunther, 210n4
Stern, David G., 216n1 (chap. 15)

Tong, Aug, 215n (chap. 13)
Twain, Mark, 91–92, 96

Unger, Peter, 209n6
Urmson, J. O., 158, 214n1 (chap. 12)

Voltaire, 189, 196, 216n9

Weber, Max, 163, 215n2 (chap. 12)
Wittgenstein, 202, 216n1 (chap. 15)
Wolf, Susan, 213n7
Wright, Crispin, 216n1 (chap. 15)

Xenophanes of Colophon, 108

Zangwill, Nick, 216n1 (chap. 15)
Zeno, 75